CREATING LITERARY STORIES:
A Fiction Writer's Guide

Creating
LITERARY STORIES:

A Fiction Writer's Guide

by WILLIAM H. COLES

First edition

Published January 2016

Story in Literary Fiction
99 West South Temple #1802
Salt Lake City, Utah 84101

www.storyinliteraryfiction.com

Cover art by Casey Childs
Cover and interior design by Susanne Howard

ISBN: 978-0-9961903-6-7 (softcover)
ISBN: 978-0-9961903-7-4 (hardcover)
ISBN: 978-0-9961903-8-1 (ebook)

TABLE OF CONTENTS

CHAPTER 2

Character in a Literary Fictional Story

Development

Character is everything in literary fiction. Character does not replace plot and setting or theme and meaning, but character intimately relates to all of those. In literary fiction, every character needs complexities and uniquenesses that may or may not be actually written on the page. Two-dimensional, flat characters are often necessary and useful in storytelling, but there should be the depth of three dimensions for all characters in the creator's mind. Depth of understanding of all characters ensures that underlying motivations are reasonable, dialogue is believable, and logic of action is clear through innovative character development and well-crafted plots.

Fiction is less reliant on the discovery of something already known than on the awareness of how and why something happens based on character and plot. In biography and autobiography, the character is formed before the writing starts. The author chooses descriptions of happenings and there are few decisions allowing change for the betterment of the story.

Complexity

The goal of character creation in fiction is complex, but creating a unique character—one that is not stereotypical—is the essence of great fictional stories. The characters will be adopted by the reader and drive the momentum of the plot. At the start of character development, there are no restrictions to character description or action. A character emerges unencumbered. Then that character in fiction is shaped for credible plot development. The character must be unique, but remain believable and within the boundaries set by the suspension of disbelief all fiction requires. The character must not be stereotypical, and must feel comfortable or familiar to the reader. As a memorable character develops, the reader becomes attached to and admires the character in the same way they would begin to think of a new acquaintance as a friend. This reader attachment is often associated with liking the character, but liking is not absolutely necessary and respect and/or admiration without liking can also be strong pathways to a reader's attachment to a character.

As the author creates an emerging character, subtle choices and imaginative attributes must keep within the overall story guidelines set in the contract between author and reader. In revision, scenes, thoughts, actions, conflicts, and motivations that do not contribute maximally to the character engaging the reader and driving the plot forward should be changed or eliminated.

Maximizing opportunities

To create a character for a reader in a literary story, there are a limited number of things the character can think or do. In a short story, even for the protagonist, there may be only ten to twenty key characterization opportunities. Often, there are fewer. In a novel, with its longer timeline and wider range of development from the direct storyline, there are more opportunities for a character to show his or her true colors, but ultimately even these openings are limited. How do authors recognize key opportunities and make the most of them? First, character development must be reasonable for the story and for the sensibilities of the reader. The actions and thoughts of the character must also be unique, with elements of surprise, so that they embed in the reader's memory. Showing a character's actions, thoughts, and opinions in-scene has more lasting impact than narrative telling. And character development leaves a greater impression on the reader when in-scene story time predominates over backstory or the narrator's comments on past character actions.

Misconceptions

Literary fiction demands extraordinary skills in the realm of character development. Authors must learn and practice the art of creating characters—skillful characterization is not inherent in every writer—and not accept the often-taught dictum that characters take over the author's stories when the author is in his or her best writing trance. The idea that the character carries the story to successful completion is a common but surefire limitation to developing the best fictional characters. Characters are imagined and created—not discovered and described—in a maximally effective story. And never are great characters conjured from unthinking trances.

Significance

Stories, to be great, should be significant and meaningful. A major way for an author to instill these qualities in storytelling is through effective characterization and valuable thinking that surprises and enlightens.

Although many would instinctively disagree, it is true that memoir, creative nonfiction, and biography do not have the options and do not reach the potential of character development available to the fiction writer. Yet the vast majority of fiction stories today are simply tales by authors relating something that happened to them or someone they know, and calling the result fiction. A character's traits are described. This result does not have the imaginative structure of fiction, and often relies on narrative telling to the reader rather than in-scene engagement and creative excitement. It is through story creation that fiction can reach a unique excellence and significance.

Stereotypes

Stereotypes abound in many stories, and are often essential. Comic superheroes are notoriously rigid; for Spiderman and the like, those writing their adventures must adhere strictly to the visual and story history so familiar to the reader. Hercule Poirot, Agatha Christie's detective, is consistent crime after crime; he has a role that defines him and that is required for the storytelling as she created it.

In literary fiction, every character, by nature of the creative process, emerges from the author's imagination stereotypical, and is then developed to some non-stereotypical threshold. This builds reader interest and augments the quality of the story. But in stories with multiple characters, all characters cannot be unique, vibrant, and memorable; some stereotypes are unavoidable. This is not bad. Overdevelopment of too many characters may create unbelievable and/or ineffective fiction. As in the writing of all fiction, a proper balance must be sought—a balance that is unique and suited to each writer's style and sensibilities.

Character-based plot

A character-based story, with character strengths and weaknesses contributing to plot progression, is one way, if not the best way, to achieve theme and meaning.

Here is a story that has lasted for more than 150 years, "Little Red Riding Hood." It serves as an example of how to clarify the meaning of character-based story.

> *Once upon a time, in a village near the deep dark woods, was a girl named Little Red Riding Hood. She wants to take Grandma, who is ill, a basket of goodies. Red will have to walk through the woods for half an hour to get to Grandma's house, which is in another village. "Be careful," Red's mother says. "Go straight on the path and do not talk to strangers." Little Red goes into the woods and meets a wolf who wants to eat her but can't because there is a woodsman nearby. The wolf asks where she's going and whom she will visit. Red tells all. The wolf runs off and Red continues her journey. She fails to heed her mother's warning about staying on the path and leaves it to chase butterflies, pick bluebells, and dip her toe in a cold, refreshing stream. When she gets to Grandma's house, the wolf has already arrived; he imitates Red's voice to gain entrance, then devours Grandma, dresses in Grandma's nightclothes, and crawls in bed. Little Red arrives. He tells her to come in. As the wolf exposes himself little by little, Red listens to his smooth talk then she asks him about his big eyes, hairy arms, and teeth. Unsuspecting, she gets in bed and he devours her.*

What has kept this story in the collective consciousness for so long? First, it carries three significant messages: 1) listen to your parents, 2) innocence and naïveté can cause irreversible harm, and 3) don't trust a stranger, especially in grandma's clothing; it can be fatal. There is also the effective metaphor of the wolf as a child predator.

But look how the significance of the story is mainly carried by the narrative structure. The story is character-based because of Red's human characteristics, especially her human foibles: she holds onto her child-hood innocence, she disobeys her mother, she talks to strangers even when warned not to.

This story could be framed as genre fiction. It could still be interesting, but it might not be as lasting because of the structure. Here is a possibility:

> *Red Riding Hood is kidnapped from the woods near her house. A few hours later some bones and scraps of skin are found at her grandmother's house a mile away. The police are called in, and they discover from the gray hairs trapped in grandma's hand-woven throw rug that the wolf did it. The wolf escapes. Red's mother grieves at Red's funeral, praying for quick justice.*

This version is a statement of happenings. Red is a part of the plot, but she is not driving the plot by disobeying her mother and wallowing in her innocence. And the wolf metaphor loses its power when the story moves from fantasy to a more reality-based police procedural.

Here is another possible genre framework for the story, that of action-adventure:

> *Red decides to go to Grandma's house for a visit. In the deep, dark forest she meets a woodsman who is tracking a wolf that has eaten two children in recent weeks. Red wants to help find the culprit. The woodsman agrees and sends her out as a decoy. The wolf tries to attack Red, but she stabs him with a knife the woodsman gave her. The wolf runs away, but the woodsman follows the trail of blood. He finds the wolf near Grandma's house, and, after a life-threatening duel, the wolf is killed. Red falls in love with the woodsman.*

In this story, again, all that happens in the plot is circumstantial. Who Red really is makes little difference. What she says, thinks, or wants is irrelevant. The same story could be written, with minor changes, with Pinocchio as the major character.

An author could restructure so that Red's decisions *do* drive the plot to become more character-based again, but in another way. And the story gains character-based meaning:

Red Riding Hood's grandma, who lives in another village, is very rich and has a new dress, a box of Swiss chocolates, and bath oil waiting for Red Riding Hood for her birthday party the following week. But Red wants her presents now, even though her mother tells her to wait until next week, when her father can accompany her through the woods, which can be very dangerous; there are evil strangers lurking there. But Red goes anyway to get her presents early, meets the wolf in the forest, and befriends him. She and Grandma are devoured.

Here Red is driving the plot again, and there is significant meaning related to Red's human attributes—greed and impatience along with innocence and the failure to obey—that can be fatal.

Writers seeking to write great literary fiction can take two important points from the Red Riding Hood story: 1) structure the story to demonstrate what it means to be human through character-based plotting, and 2) make the story significant. In Red's case, the significance is partially related to the dire consequences of getting eaten by a wolf after seemingly innocuous actions but contrary to conventional wisdom.

Summary

The author who wants to create great stories must characterize well. Time and multiple attempts are required, and a healthy dissatisfaction with all early opportunities is essential. Authors must never be satisfied with mediocrity.

CHAPTER 3

Narration of Literary Stories

To successfully narrate a story in fiction, authors must know what words mean and not confuse terms or use them interchangeably. Note in particular the difference in meanings between *narrative* the noun versus *narrative* the adjective; *narrator* versus *character*; and *literary fiction* versus *memoir*.

Narrate v: to give an account of something in detail

Narrator n: somebody who tells a story or gives an account of something

Character n: one of the people portrayed in a story

Narration n: the act of telling a story or giving an account of something

Narrative (1) n: an account of a sequence of events in the order in which they happened

Narrative (2) n: a discussion or speech about the policies, opinions, or proposals of a political party (e.g., the senator's narrative…)

Narrative adj: having the aim or purpose of telling a story, or involving the art of storytelling

Point of View (POV) (1) n: position in relation to a story being told

Point of View (POV) (2) n: how someone or something is observed

Point of View (POV) (3) n: position or attitude in considering a matter

Author n: the creator or originator of something

Fiction n: stories that describe imaginary people and events

Literary fiction n: serious, character-based fiction (as opposed to genre or popular fiction, which are plot based)

Story n: an account of a series of events

Memoir n: an account of real events written from personal knowledge

Autobiography n: an account of someone's life written by that person

Biography n: an account of someone's life written by another person

Creative nonfiction n: literary or narrative journalism using literary skills

Written literary fictional stories that are loved and remembered are almost always: 1) imagined and created by an author, 2) told by a narrator created by the author but usually as a separate "narrator" intellect speaking from a unique worldview and experience of his/her individual personality, and often speaking from a different time than the story time or the author's time in writing the story, and 3) acted out by characters imagined by the author for the story (although these may often be inspired—but not copied—from events or characters in real life).

Narrative perspective

Narration means telling a story. Writers are taught today that there are three points of view (POVs) from which one can deliver a story:

first-person POV: the "I" approach
second-person POV: the "you" and "we" approach
third-person POV: the "he" and "she" approach

But there may also be a *narrator point of view*. This point of view is often not identified, and it may deliver information out of scene and even out of story. The narrator may be speaking from other than the story's time, and voice, ideation, syntax, and word usage may be different than the characters'. Narrator perspectives are often essential and should be consistent, established early in the story, and under the author's control.

When an author creates a narrator for a story, it is possible to 1) establish story truth from real-world truth and credibility, 2) discover opportunities for irony and enlightenment, 3) enhance humor in the telling (especially irony), and 4) demand that the author learn the broadest worldview and in-depth understanding of humanity for plot and characterization. The talented use of narrator perspective in a literary story, separate from the author, provides opportunities for excellence.

Narration is a complex understanding for a writer and necessary for high-quality storytelling. The essential question is: who is telling the story at what time in the story? It's not just the POV. Careful analysis in any "point of view" may show different authors, often unknowingly, telling stories with or without distinct narrators from multiple minds through multiple personas, real or imagined—all identifiable by the reader. Consider these perspectives in telling a story: 1) the author directly tells the story with his or her voice, persona, and worldview, 2) the author creates a story that is told through a distinct narrator presence, either identified or not, taking that narrator's voice, persona, and worldview, and 3) the author chooses to tell the story through a single character using only that character's voice, persona, and worldview. In modern fiction, all of these perspectives, and even mixtures of them, are used.

Why is narrative perspective important? Isn't understanding point of view sufficient? Great, memorable fiction stories that stay popular among future generations are quite rare, and the authors who create such stories have unique and varied attributes. What trait seems to drive writers to create stories of great significance and sustainability? Look to Austen, Homer, Forster, Conrad, Flaubert, Chekhov, De Maupassant, Babel, Melville, Hawthorne, Munro. The great storytellers, with few exceptions, write selflessly to engage and entertain the reader, and the quality of the story produced offers significant enlightenment regarding life and being human.

Lesser writers are intent on fame and fortune and the seriously mistaken belief that to be great it is sufficient to write solely for catharsis, self-aggrandizement, and ego. These writers create "literature of self" that often ignores: 1) an in-depth understanding of humanity, 2) a broad, objective incorporation of the world outside an author's worldview, 3) respect for a reader's gracious exertion in reading, and 4) new thoughts about human existence in the world. Literary stories are more than simply retellings of what happened; literary stories also reflect character change.

Memoir, autobiography, authorial-dominated "fiction," and creative nonfiction all are contributions to literature, but the imaginative, created fictional story reaches unique excellence. Understanding the complexities of narration and developing narrative skills through practice represent an important start on the path to great fictional storytelling.

Readers benefit from the use of accurate narrative perspective at appropriate times. Narrative perspective helps define what is true, credible, and reliable in the story world and guides the reader's understanding, emotional acceptance, and involvement in the literary story. In many stories, narrative perspective allows eventual comparison and application by the reader to his or her real-world existence.

Adherence to effective narration is essential for success in literary storytelling.

Objective delivery of a story

Objectivity in storytelling by the narrator creates a story experience told in a nonjudgmental, truthful, and credible way. It's in the voice, the story structure—in ideation with truth, morality, and credibility of storytelling. Of course, the plot can still be rife with lies, evil, false everythings, questionable will, desires, and betrayals. That's what stories are made of. But the story delivery should be objective, so that, knowing all the facts, readers are engaged and make their own decisions about the story. It is important that readers not be bludgeoned with biased "truths" and absolute thinking in the storytelling through ineffective narration. Readers should be guided to their own conclusions about theme and meaning through excellent characterization and objective plotting that is unbiased by the author's feelings and structured to engage the reader in the story such that his or her own opinions are formed and new thinking is stimulated.

Narrative distance: physical, psychological

A good story benefits from narrative perspective that has been incorporated into the writer's storytelling style. For example, a scene at a U.S. Civil War battle scene may benefit from the POV of a commanding general overlooking the conflict from a high vantage point *and* the POVs of soldiers fighting for their lives where the view of the action is limited to a few yards. This would relate to physical perspective in a specific POV but also provide alternatives in the psychological perspective. The general's heavy responsibility and distance from immediate death makes his emotions and psychological mindset different from an on-the-battlefield soldier terrified of dying young and never knowing love or wisdom, filled with feelings of inadequacy regarding his battle skills and wondering why he's been chosen for this carnage. These narrative considerations can be extremely useful to an author, and the POVs provide alternatives of seeing through characters with careful attention to narrative perspective.

In-scene versus narrative telling

Authors must clarify their own thinking about how to provide story information: 1) story advanced by telling a sequence of events, 2) in-scene reader involvement by showing character action, 3) descriptive narrative, 4) dialogue, 5) images and setting.

Show-don't-tell has been the imperative in literary fiction for centuries, but fewer and fewer authors comply. The result is fewer good stories created as an art form.

Point of view

Narrators use character points of view to tell a story. The first person and the third person are the most commonly used. (Second person is trendy but rarely provides the lasting reader satisfaction necessary for great storytelling.) The narrator has a point of view that may be used for improving time management of story progression, or for relating information that is not within the reasonable range of the character's senses, memory (life experiences), education, or intelligence.

Point of view has many definitions. Most commonly writers think of point of view as a position in space, time, or development from which something is considered. But point of view can also be a manner of evaluating something, or a reasoned opinion about something.

In essence, a character point of view is not simply a position for considering physical action in a story. It is character-revealing way for the narrator to present story information to the reader. And there are complexities of point of view that, if not appreciated or if mismanaged, will cause the reader to unnecessarily question the character's reliability and credibility. It is not helpful to think of a point of view in storytelling as a camera, as is often taught. Evaluating story action and opinions—things a camera does not do—are also involved. This broad, multi-definition approach to point of view is especially useful when considering use of narrator and character points of view together.

> *I despised Amy. She was beautiful, I'll give her that, but she thought the world revolved around her—that God made other people to admire her. Never once did she think of me, or anyone, as a human with feelings.*

The structure of this paragraph is common, and acceptable to many readers, but what Amy thought and wanted is not within reasonable boundaries of the first-person point of view. Of course it's speculation, but is it true? How effective is first-person speculation in building Amy's character when it might not be true? With a different narrative structure, the reader can learn reliable information about Amy. From the narrator.

> *Jason despised Amy even though he was enamored with her beauty. Amy believed God made other humans to admire her and Jason longed for the slightest sign Amy knew he was alive. But she never thought of him.*

Information provided through a character—first or third person—that is not reasonable makes that character unreliable, either intentionally or unintentionally. A character does not know the truth of Amy's thoughts, and also shows arrogance in telling the reader these impossibilities. These may not be aspects of the character the author wants to imply. It is sometimes necessary to use a first-person character as a more story story-wise narrator. But it must not be accidental, and it must be consistent within the story being written.

In general, the if-it-works-and-I wrote-it, it-must-be-good approach to creating fictional stories is not a useful way to improve. Well-reasoned opinions about point of view are essential for all authors who want to be in control of the storytelling process.

Voice

Voice and point of view, although related, are not the same. Voice is everything a character does and says that helps identify the character. Point of view is the microscopic (close) or telescopic (distant) way a narrator delivers story information. And while characters deliver story information in their own voices, a narrator-voice may actually be telling the story—even in the first person—through either character voice or narrator-distinct voice.

Thinking of the oral tradition when writing

In academic discussions and workshops, terms are frequently used without a common understanding as to their meaning. As a result, entire careers have been riddled with confusion about the basics of storytelling and the unique problems inherent in the written story. It is helpful, in discussions of point of view and narrators, to think of an oral storytelling tradition. The storyteller is always telling the story. The teller is often not the author of the story, and is in control of narrative passages, action, dialogue, and internal reflection.

At times, the storyteller relies on suspension of disbelief—that the storyteller could know the information presented—to increase tension and infuse drama. And listeners can have transcendence as if they were within the characters' living selves. Imagine Ornesto, a storyteller, relating Henry James's *The Turn of the Screw* to a high school literature class in 2015. James published the story in 1898. Ornesto, to be effective in his dramatization, will make the presentation as familiar to his contemporary audience as possible; given a story already open to decades of interpretations, he will tell it in his way. He might dip into Flora's or Miles's mind, choosing most relevant facts for his purpose, or characterize Mrs. Grose with room left for the 2015 listeners to fill in their own details. Ornesto will make Peter Quint as evil as he can, choosing his words carefully (mostly if not all from James) for the best effect.

Ornesto is the narrator; he knows all about the story world and chooses story facts from a limited story-world perspective. (Henry James is considered the creator of the story world, with knowledge outside the story world.) Note that as narrator, Ornesto will make the best choices about story information for his audience. It is this advantage of separation between author, narrator, and character(s) that is available but that fiction writers often ignore. Ornesto, to keep his story moving effectively, will narrate, and may well use different points of view than what the author Henry James would.

Here is a useful rule: the fiction author writes the story, but should not tell the story. The narrator tells the story (that is created by the author) and contributes to story from within the limits of the story world. And the narrator may use the narrator's voice for certain story information, and uses character point of view—or points of view—and voice to deliver other story content. In addition, when using a character point of view, the narrator may use the character's voice, persona, worldview, and life experience, either partially or pervasively. This is story delivery with narrative perspective.

There are two difficult concepts to digest: 1) by a clear conceptualization of author-narrator-character-delivered information, authors add ease to reader understanding, and 2) when contemporary writers choose a single character's point of view exclusively, especially first person, as if it were a selective filter, they often limit the potential of the story.

Thinking of stage-play dramatization when writing

In almost every sense, writers of stories have at their disposal many different tools for the narration of stories. Writing a drama for stage is different. In a stage play there are the characters whose actions and speeches deliver the story. The characters rarely directly turn to the audience to deliver narrator-specific information. The exceptions are worthy of study. William Shakespeare often has a narrator on stage, perhaps in character, delivering a monologue or soliloquy. Here is an example.

> To be, or not to be- that is the question:
> Whether 'tis nobler in the mind to suffer
> The slings and arrows of outrageous fortune
> Or to take arms against a sea of troubles,
> And by opposing end them. To die- to sleep-
> No more; and by a sleep to say we end
> The heartache, and the thousand natural shocks

That flesh is heir to. 'Tis a consummation
Devoutly to be wish'd. To die- to sleep.
To sleep- perchance to dream: ay, there's the rub!
For in that sleep of death what dreams may come
When we have shuffled off this mortal coil,
Must give us pause. There's the respect
That makes calamity of so long life.

William Shakespeare, *Hamlet* act III, scene 1

What glorious and significant thoughts but delivered outside the action of the play. In essence, the playwright tells theme and meaning directly to the audience. Not easily accepted in today's literary writing where theme and meaning are established through characterization and action.

Another example for awareness of narrative complexity in literature is a study of stage presentation in Thornton Wilder's *Our Town* (1938), where an actor as narrator acts in the character of a stage manager, not in the play but as an organizer of the play for the audience, and directly interacts with the audience outside the actual stage-play action. The technique is used in literary fiction too, but is not often useful to contemporary authors because it alters reader engagement and qualities of characterization and plot progression.

Narrator versus authorial intrusion

Narrators contribute to the story presentation and direct decisions about character contribution. If narrator information does not fit into the continuous fictional dream of the story provided for the reader at that moment, it is an intrusion and should not be included. Authors must use narrative techniques while remaining true to quality story-telling. Any extraneous thought, opinion, or emotion of the author in a story should be removed as detrimental to creating a story as an art form.

Author intrusion often borders on essay and propaganda and is not compatible with great fictional stories. This does not mean that themes and meanings important to the author are not an integral part of great stories. They are. But they are expressed through careful story structure and skillful, craft-savvy presentation.

In the main, however, it is important that authorial morality be understood, and be consistent. All good literary stories are constructed on a moral framework that defines character and narrator morality. Moral principles are the cardiovascular system of a literary fictional story.

Close (or tight) versus distant character points of view

The reader's sense of how close the character is to the story action is created by syntax, word choice, and ideation. This is true in all delivery choices for story including presentation, dialogue, narration, description, internal reflection, and even exposition.

As a character seems more distant from the action, he or she functions more as a narrator. The author who recognizes character and narrator information in close and distant terms is able to present more effective voicings, more in-depth character reliability, and more easily grasped imagery, and will be in better control of the writing process.

First-person POV and narrator POV

In first-person narration, in in-scene construction of a story passage, to be accurate, the first person can only tell and comment on what is happening in the story within the range of his or her five senses in the character's memory at the moment in the story time. Along the same line, if the first person comments on the past, it has to be within the intellectual capabilities and memory for story events, and when speculating, within the characters' capabilities and established sensitivities.

But narrators are different. Every narrator tells about something that has happened, that is from a period where time has progressed, knowledge has increased, history expanded, understanding explored. For a reader to accept information outside the logical thoughts and perceptions of the first-person character, the reader must believe that the first-person character is older and looking back on the story—and that the first person is wiser and acting as a narrator—or accept a narrator's contribution to the story as created by the author to help the reader understand the story. This takes considerable skill and failure leads to inferior writing.

The narrator's point of view is not a silo in a field of character-point-of-view silos. Narrators tell stories, and it is not useful to consider a narrator point of view as similar to—or equivalent to—a character's point of view. Narrators float above the story in a sort of hot-air balloon with useful overviews that characters cannot achieve.

Omniscient (knowing everything) narrator: Narrators know only about their story worlds. They know more than is told in the story by the characters, but they do not know all that the author knows, and they should not tell what the author knows and believes outside the story world. This is an important distinction for an author who wants to tell stories clearly, logically, and effectively.

Story world: The story world is restricted, selective, purposeful, intense, directed, and never random. It is where the characters act, and it is what the narrator delivers to the reader. In good fiction, its boundaries are sacrosanct and should not be violated.

Narrator epiphany: Usually characters change because of revelations or changes in the way they think about something, brought about by story action. In general, narrators tell stories and do not change significantly. But there are exceptions. Many stories have very effective narrators blessed with revelations and reversals in thinking that may or may not be similar to those of a character. How characters and sometimes narrators change in a story needs to be under the author's constant consideration before and during writing, and in revision.

Timeline and point of view: A character's point of view changes with the advancement of the story time (as does that of every living human). There are three elements of point of view, all of which are a part of our understanding of the concept: position in space or time, a mental attitude or opinion, and a manner of evaluating.

Multiple third-person points of view equals omniscient point of view

Points of view in a story are not spices in a stew that give a blended effect. Points of view are pears, figs, cashews, and marshmallows all in a bowl that are consumed separately with sometimes memorable and always distinct individual effects that contribute to the whole experience of eating. Omniscient point of view is not a term equal to multiple points of view, but it is often implied as equal in discussions of the craft of writing. And for excellence in storytelling, authors should consider narrative perspective and create identifiable narrator and characters through individual, identifiable POVs, voice, persona, worldview, and life experiences.

CHAPTER 4

Dialogue

Great dialogue in literary fiction serves multiple functions but never detracts from the story's progress or purpose. Take this example from classic literature, which has action, conflict, revelation, and voice. It serves multiple purposes:

> *"If I were in heaven, Nelly, I should be extremely miserable."*
>
> *"Because you are not fit to go there," I answered. "All sinners would be miserable in heaven."*
>
> *"But it is not for that. I dreamt once that I was there."*
>
> *"I tell you I won't harken to your dreams, Miss Catherine! I'll go to bed," I interrupted again.*
>
> *She laughed, and held me down; for I made a motion to leave my chair.*
>
> *"This is nothing," cried she: "I was only going to say that heaven did not seem to be my home; and I broke my heart with weeping to come back to earth."*

Emily Brontë, *Wuthering Heights*

Basic rules of dialogue

In fiction, successful dialogue serves one, and usually more, of the following purposes:

- advances the story
- develops characters
- moves the plot
- illuminates a theme or meaning
- provides a time transition (usually subtle)
- changes the direction of the plot, usually through conflict
- creates voice and tone, for story or for characters
- provides understanding of enlightenment for characters

- illuminates desire and motivation
- supports attribution with consistent syntax and ideation
- meets the rhythmic necessity of human speech compatible with story dialogue
- adds drama (through conflict and resultant action)
- provides movement for story ideas and plot

In fiction, successful dialogue (almost) never:

- is used only to break up a narrative passage
- tells what was actually said in an author's experience
- provides exposition that questions credibility in any way
- is static prose
- provides prose context for a clever simile or metaphor
- slows down story-plot movement
- provides a setting that is better conveyed via narrative
- addresses author opinion
- mimics what a character might say in the real world
- is a conversation in quotes without story-related purpose

In great fiction, dialogue is not intuitive, and it does not come naturally to writers. Most importantly, for effective dialogue in fiction, authors cannot simply describe a conversation from real experience or from an imagined scene. Dialogue must always serve the purpose of story development; therefore, it cannot be a taped recording of reality. In revision of dialogue, these questions are useful:

Is dialogue *logical*?
Does it fit character *desire* and *motivation*?
Does it support *theme* and *meaning*?
Does it *move*?

Ideas for improvement of dialogue

A. Characters

Consider dialogue from the character's story "reality." When revising a specific dialogue segment, ask:

-Is it logical for the character's *education*?
-Is it true to story time and the character's *age*?
-Does it match the character's *emotion* of the moment?

-Does it fit the character's credible *thinking* and *perceptions* of the moment?

B. Avoid authorial thinking

Writing literary fiction is objective. Author ideas and opinions should not drive dialogue unless they are consistent with the characters and narrator and serve a purpose in the story.

Characters climbing into a life raft in a churning sea after the cruise ship sank.

> *"My leg is broken."*
> *"Where's Ernest?*
> *"Is there a flare?"*
> *"There ought to be criminal charges for crews getting into lifeboats before paying passengers."*

The last quote is authorial. It's a concept out of the moment and expressing ideas illogical for a moment of crisis.

C. Avoid direct answers (kills movement)

> *"Is that a Gila monster?"*
> *"Yes, I think it is."*

The above is not usable dialogue. It fills time and space on the page, but it does nothing for drama or story. What about:

> *"Stay back, they bite!"*

But this has no realism. When nothing is working, look for a greater problem. Should the idea even be expressed in dialogue at all?

Let's think about this for a minute. "Is that a Gila monster?" may not be direct character dialogue that is useful in any story. The dialogue is being used to inform the reader of the presence of a potentially dangerous creature. In dramatic fiction, a scene must have a purpose, and it must have action. "Is that a Gila monster?" has no effect in fiction; it sounds contrived, and it lacks dramatic conflict between the character(s) and the forces of nature (monster). Realistically, the dialogue speaker must be afraid, or planning escape, or figuring out a way to kill the enemy, or admiring its unusually threatening size. But will that work? A key revision might be to remove this information from dialogue.

D. Avoid "talking heads" (two-character ping-pong dialogue)

Although frequently necessary, dialogue limited to two characters (or even talking to oneself in an internal monologue) can become dreadfully boring. Conflict is essential in every dialogue passage to maintain the necessary energy for the dialogue segment. Creating dialogue takes practice:

> **Agreement**
> *"That bull is a pussycat."*
> *"I don't know why they put it in the draw."*

> **Conflict inserted**
> *"That bull is a pussycat."*
> *"You don't know nothin'. He damn near killed Prettyboy. Knocked him out for two days."*

> **More characters provide more information, with conflict**
> *"That bull is a pussycat."*
> *"Well, he knocked out Prettyboy."*
> *"You shouldn't put him in the draw, anyway. No reason to get mangled by some crazy man killer."*
> *"Comes from a family of good bulls. Wish I had more like him."*

E. Avoid simile and metaphor

Never rely on hard-and-fast rules to guide your dialogue creation, but do beware of simile and metaphor. It is often impossible to find the right simile that fits into the context of a dialogue segment and is appropriate and credible with respect to the character's intelligence and experience. An extreme example:

> *"Ignore her," she said. "She looks like Marie Antoinette with a sex change."*

This is dialogue created by an author who is trying to be clever and failing because the simile conjures no specific imagery.

"She looks like hell."

Even if the author argues that this is in the vernacular of the character and helps define him or her, the simile is a cliché and adds nothing to the writing. Any metaphor that calls attention to itself in dialogue should be deleted.

Creating conflict in dialogue

SCENE: a twin-engine propeller plane at 7,000 feet, the fuselage door open, a woman in her late thirties with a parachute strapped to her back, about to jump; an instructor is visible behind her.

Draft 1.

"Don't do it."
"I won't."
"It's one of the most difficult maneuvers we have in skydiving."
"I've never wanted to take the risk."

There is no conflict here, despite the opportunity for it. This is totally static writing, and not credible. The pacing is wrong for the content. Purpose for the dialogue is not clear. And it contains exposition (about skydiving).

Draft 2.

"Don't do it."
"It's why I came."
"Think of Janie and Sally."
"No time to think of my children."

The exposition about children is inappropriate for this story scenario. If the children's names are already in story, this is redundant, and even if not previously introduced, the mention of children is not logical if someone is about to jump out of an airplane; that is, it is not a useful response to a fictional situation. In fiction dialogue, the emotion at the time of the jump must be strong and felt by the reader through the dialogue. No sense of emotion comes through in this dialogue, making any discussion of children unlikely. Note that for the experienced skydiver, jumping out of a plane might be an everyday experience that would allow discussion about children, but rarely, and it would take careful construction.

Draft 3.

"The ripcord won't work."
"You're saying that to scare me."
"It's defective."
"You packed it."

Some conflict here, which is an improvement. But this is not usable dialogue. Purpose must relate to story, and purpose must be the right choice for a dialogue segment. Clearly the author, in creating this dialogue, had confused purposes in mind. Is this segment about defective equipment? A desire to direct someone, to blame someone? Learning about one or both characters? And if so, learning what? A good writer demands that dialogue has a clearly identifiable purpose related to the story and the story moment in time, and does not allow defective dialogue to slip in. If this really is about defective equipment, maybe it shouldn't be in dialogue. Perhaps better in a narrative passage.

Draft 4.

"You've got less than ten seconds."
"What about you?"
"Count. Pull the cord. You've got to be clear."
"Where is your chute?"
"Five, four..."
"Where is the pin?"

"You've got to be clear" probably means clear of flying objects, including the plane. This is information no one would say—it is too obvious. This problem usually indicates a need for a narrative passage or information to be delivered in another way, possibly as internalization. Also, is "You've less than ten seconds" credible structure for dialogue? Wouldn't a character say "Hurry!"? The same revision logic goes for "Count. Pull the cord. You've got to be clear." Just "Pull the cord!" is more efficient and acceptable.

Draft 5.

"Jump."

"Not without you."

Assuming the fact that two experienced skydivers are in an in-flight emergency with one parachute is already established, there is an opportunity for learning about characters—a moment of grace.

Dialogue arouses interest

Consider this exchange:

> *"I can't believe God exists," she said.*
>
> *"There's no evidence He exists," he said, nodding. "You don't have to be a scientist to know that."*
>
> *"If you're told time after time from the moment you take your first breath that God exists, it begins to be true."*
>
> *"A fact of the mind."*
>
> *"And not in any way a fact in reality."*
>
> *"And I can't believe God ever listened to me pray."*
>
> *"Me either. And I don't believe He ever intervened in my life, in one way or the other."*
>
> *"And how can there be a heaven? The sky is unfathomable, infinite. There can't be some floating gardens and Saint Paul at a golden gate with God sitting in an aluminum folding chair trimming his beard with cuticle scissors," he said, laughing.*
>
> *"And no hell!"*
>
> *"Maybe hell is here on Earth."*
>
> *"Feels like it sometimes, doesn't it?"*
>
> *"Does it ever."*

A major responsibility of an author creating fiction dialogue is to engage the reader's interest. In the main, an author does this with conflict, surprising information, revelations about something, advancing the plot, evoking images, or providing ideas that provoke thought and wonder. This segment does not do that. Even the humor is awkward; it's not story related. The discussion is bland and tedious, and the sound of the dialogue doesn't sound true to a story exchange between two characters.

The purpose of this dialogue is not to entertain, either; it's to establish the idea that God doesn't exist. Successful literary fiction is entertaining. This is boring and without conflict. Do you believe the characterization is enhanced by this exchange? Don't they sound like muddy thinkers without an ounce of originality, their thoughts encased in cliché like a pistachio nut in its shell?

And do you get the slightest sense that any reader will have of new awareness about God or a change in thinking, experience increased attachment to the characters, or care much what the next dialogue segment will bring? This is unsuccessful dialogue in fiction. In essence, the segment has not been conceived and constructed to move the plot, characterize, enlighten the reader, or entertain through quality of prose to stimulate and move ideas.

About sound

Writers often spend years seeking the right sound for their dialogue. Sound is important, but only when the dialogue fulfills a primary purpose of doing something important for the story. To be aware of the sound, it may help to read out loud—and if you're really serious, record and listen to yourself. Always remember that dialogue in fiction is not the way people speak, yet, paradoxically, it has to *seem* to be the way people speak. How to do that? First, there has to be a natural rhythm to the context in which the speech is carried out. If dialogue is related to an audience with the Pope, speech patterns will differ from those in a bar conversation with Jelly Roll Morton. When writing, notice how the same content can have incredibly varied rhythmic presentations. Create alternatives, and choose the best one(s) for your writing and the story. Musicality is more important in some styles than others; it is always present, but it must not dominate when the story-purpose of dialogue might be lost.

A final thought

The challenge of creating your own effective dialogue will not come from copying some writer you love to read. Of course, read and learn. And then practice. But in the long run, you will need to make decisions about dialogue in your stories. These decisions—essential for voice, movement, clarity, purpose, and credibility—are based on how you think about and create fictional stories, and can only be solved by you. You are the creator, and when you succeed, your writing will be well received, and you will have found your own unique style.

CHAPTER 5

Conflict in Literary Fiction

Conflict is the essence of drama, and all literary fiction requires drama to please the reader and make the story succeed. At the story's core, conflict is the momentum of happening and change and is crucial on all levels for delivering information and building characterization. Conflict as a source of change that engages a reader, and in a story, conflict and action, deliver what descriptions of feelings and situations cannot.

The best storytellers have a knack for engaging readers, bringing them inside the skin of the story. Readers are carried through a story with a succession of related conflicts. But many contemporary authors seemingly lack the ability or desire to use action and conflict. There is an increasing habit to tell stories about *me*—my thoughts, my life, my accomplishments—often under the guise of fiction. The literature-of-self. But for lasting success—a story that will persist into the future of great literature as an art form—creative-fiction authors should strive to express most of their story ideas with drama and conflict, and not as authorial catharsis.

In life, everything tends toward inertia. Throw a rock into the air, it falls to the ground and lies motionless. Pour water into a glass, it settles and becomes still. We are born, we are active, but we are always moving toward the solitude and inaction of motionless death. In fiction, writers succumb to this natural tendency to write stories that seek a state of inertia, a state where nothing happens. This is especially noticeable when a story relies on a narrative description of past events rather than dramatic action scenes. It is avoided by in-scene and in-the-moment action, by learning how to instill conflict in narrative that relentlessly presses on toward resolution or no resolution, and by assuring that conflict is embedded in all aspects of the prose. A few strategies:

Be dramatic. Drama (conflict-action-resolution) *is* storytelling, and in fiction dramatic elements are necessary to move the reader sentence by sentence, idea by idea. Drama provides the tension.

Use language with conflict and energy. The beauty of language is enhanced when motion and conflict are incorporated into the prose to maintain a reader's interest word by word. In writing, the reader's mind is active in creating and forming images. Authors shouldn't create still-life images, but paint portraits and scenes that intrigue and engage with feelings and momentum—scenes that come to life on the page. "The horse jumped the wall." Static. "The stallion cleared the wall by inches landing in the mud." Improved with some action. "The horse, his steamy breath dissipating in the frigid air, left the ground, the muscles of his back legs immense in contraction, and he cleared the stone wall by inches to land in the shallow pool of muddy water, the splash soaking the britches of his cowering rider." Overwritten, but a lot of energy.

Choose energetic words. Some nouns have life and motion, and some don't.

> Sparrow. Nail. Butterfly. Comet. Ocean. Atom. Building. Pebble. Tadpole. Vacuum. Hurricane. Skeleton. Flame. Puddle.

Can you identify those that are animate versus inanimate, moving versus motionless? Life is movement and change—and the conflict it implies.

Descriptions of animate things, rather than inanimate ones, is always better for the story in fiction. In general, description (and exposition) should be buried in action for maximum effect.

Beware the burned-out effect inanimate objects create on the page. One aid is to use an inanimate object with modification that can imply motion (and impending conflict). Some examples:

> hand / trembling hand;
> man / man in declining years;
> car / race car;
> gun / Gatlin gun

Action can be implied by changing the general to the specific:

soil / muck
meteor / shooting star
spice / cilantro
horse / thoroughbred
painting / hunt scene

And in the language, it is always wise to strive for motion when the story and pacing allow it (i.e., no drivel; write only what counts for the story).

He sat in the chair.

This might be improved, space permitting. The following has action, imagery, and information:

He put his hands back for support, bent his knees, and painfully lowered himself into the wheelchair.

Consider syntax and conflict. Syntax, and how ideas are delivered, can change the energy of a sentence, often by clarifying the conflict. Let's explore various ways to get a basic message across: Grandpa killed Granny.

At the funeral and for years after, grandfather never mentioned the day he hammered granny to her grave.

The construction—past, distance, telling—gives a fait accompli tone that might not serve well.

Grandfather killed our granny.

A telling. No action.

No one was witness; we had to imagine Grandfather standing over the bed and smashing Granny's skull with a hammer before she woke.

Action is filtered through the character's imagination, but action and conflict are present because of in-the-moment construction.

Grandpa stared at the hammer as Granny's blood began to congeal with hair and fragments of skull bone.

There is in-scene action with tension present (what happened? is she dead?).

> *After he killed Granny with a hammer, Grandfather washed imagined blood off his hands every hour of the day; the skin was raw.*

In-scene action. Implied emotion of guilt. Movement. Internal conflict revealed.

> *We thought Grandfather was an intelligent man, well educated, famous in his own right. But we discovered a major flaw the night we found Granny murdered in her bed, and Grandfather laughing hysterically a few feet away.*

Telling. Lots of information. The only action here is a description of the past with Grandfather laughing. Thus, it is basically unsuccessful, its energy potential dissipated by a complicated construction.

In-scene, in-the-moment action, rather than telling, invigorates language. Note also how changing the position and content of phrases changes emphasis. In general, the basic noun/verb structure that comes last in sentence or phrase constructions is the strongest in effect. Note too that the less specific the sentence, the less effective it may be depending on context, and that complex constructions, compared to simple, terse constructions, lose energy and impact.

Build emotional conflict. In a good story, the emotions of the characters never match exactly. Even in a love story, the love interests need to be unequal—at least one of the lovers can never be sure if this is love, or there is guilt from a previous affair, and so on. Out-of-sync emotions add dramatic energy to a scene. Conflict is drama. Keep emotions changing and flowing in nature and intensity, and always relate them to the core need or desire of the character.

Internal conflict examples:

Love / hate
Sympathy / blame
Fear / sentimentality
Pliant / resistant
Understanding / unyielding

CHAPTER 7

Writing in Scene

The art of in-scene writing in fiction is critical for allowing a reader to enter the fictional story and vicariously participate in it to discover meaning and pleasure. It is one of the main skills in creating great fiction, as opposed to memoir or creative nonfiction. In-scene writing is illusory and created via a process that is difficult to dissect. *It is not narrative descriptive writing*, although certainly scenes with timelines, beginnings, middles, and ends are often created in narrative description to great effect. Narrative description tends to be static, and to increase the psychic and physical distance from the action in the scene. Not so in scene, where the writer brings the reader up close to the action, leaving space in the writing for the reader to imagine and participate.

Fourteen competencies for creating in-scene writing

1. Direct viewing with action, as if it is occurring "now" in the story time. Note the differences in these two scenes:

> *The apple fell from the lowest branch, landing in a muddy puddle too shallow to allow a splash.*

A narrator, from a distance, relating something happening.

> *The skin on his right hand blanched where he gripped the cold steel of the pistol. His left hand, bloody from the knife cut, supported his trembling right wrist.*

The third-person narrator brings immediacy, action, and intimacy through the use of the senses of the character and "close-up" imagery.

2. Switching to present tense. Changing tense has to be carefully considered, as it can be disruptive and break a well-crafted fictional dream in the reader's mind. In some circumstances, however, a switch from past to present can add immediacy and intimacy. Compare:

> *He wiped the scalpel blade on a square piece of sterile gauze. Then he cut her open, the blade engulfing itself in skin and fat until the blood oozed.*

> *He wipes the scalpel blade on a square piece of sterile gauze. The blade cuts her skin, disappearing into muscle and fat until blood oozes.*

The advantages of present tense over past are often based on taste and context. Don't switch tenses when there is minor or no improvement to be gained in the storytelling, or when the tense switch calls attention to itself. It must be seamless. In the following example, the tense change is too abrupt and distracting:

> *He was called to the OR. The patient had a distended belly. He scrubbed quickly, and wiped the scalpel blade on a square piece of sterile gauze. With a deliberate swipe the blade cuts the skin to disappear into muscle and fat until the blood oozes.*

3. Incorporating sensual detail that is attributed to a specific character, not the narrator.

> Narrator POV: *She felt the touch of his fingers on her cheek as he leaned over to kiss her ear.*

> Character third-person POV: *Her cheek knew the abrasive feel of his dry, cracked lips and her skin the exploration of her breast by his fingers seeking her always-sensitive skin, waiting to be excited.*

> Versus: POV first-person: *My cheek knew the abrasive feel of his dry cracked lips and his exploration of my skin by his fingers seeking areas he knew would excite me.*

4. Using strong verb forms. Avoid participles, which can weaken the effectiveness of action verbs in scene:

> He believed in her. (stronger)
> He was always working at believing in her. (weaker)

12. Making antecedents clear: in fiction, and especially when writing in-scene. Vague pronouns frustrate the reader. Avoid constructions such as:

> *He would never use **that** to do **this** again.*

> ***John** would never use a **spoon** to dig a **grave** again.*

In-scene writing requires clarity and authorial skill to transmit ideas without obscure imagery and question-begging syntax.

13. Minimize narrator stage direction; instead let the action set the stage. Compare:

> *He went to the door and twisted the door handle.*

> *As he opened the door, creaks from the rusty hinges alerted the fugitive.*

14. Balancing fictional style elements. Consider carefully the balance of in-scene writing versus narrative description. Both techniques are usually necessary for a successful story, and the relative use of each will vary depending on the situation. In-scene cannot deliver all that narrative can, and vice versa. Choose wisely for best development of your effective style. Think: what will it do for the reader you want to please?

A parting thought

Genre writers depend on in-scene writing. Their readers expect to be engaged in the plot and the characters' story world. In contrast, contemporary literary writers, especially academic fiction writers, seem unwilling to master in-scene writing, or willfully ignore it. Could it be a sense of superiority—the belief that writing lyrical narrative description as fiction is more intellectual? Ultimately, readers deserve only the best writing and storytelling, whether genre or literary. And every story needs a carefully considered balance of fictional elements, with in-scene and narrative description being among the most important styles of storytelling.

CHAPTER 8

The First-Person POV in the Literary Story

Most fiction writers are successful without exploring the intricacies of the first-person POV. But to achieve excellent character development in a story with a character-based plot, authors should understand how characters affect readers, and then deploy the effects through controlled writing. (Note that "first person" refers to the "I" pronoun usage in a prose story, but the "I" character may not be the protagonist, or even a major character, and may or may not be the narrator.)

Mastering first-person POV

The first-person point of view comes with disadvantages and advantages, which will vary in importance according to the story structure, content, and, of course, the abilities of the author.

ADVANTAGES

-In a narrative telling of a story to a reader, the first-person POV creates the sense of having been there (or being there in the present tense), and a memoir quality of telling the story as the straight scoop to you, the reader. Emotional and physical closeness to the action provokes intimacy.

-First-person POV gives the reader constant characterization—that is, access to the thoughts and actions of the "I" character. All other characters, even if the protagonist is not the "I" character, are secondary because of limited access to their thoughts and actions. This consistent access to one character's opinions and attitudes often strengthens voice, and allows easier access to sarcasm and cynicism, and to the injection of surprise-humor.

-First-person POV flows more easily into an intuitive writing style, allowing a certain freedom from the necessity of structure.

DISADVANTAGES

-In the first person, the acceptance of a character's dialogue changes. The reader knows that all of the other characters' statements are being presented, and might be altered in voice, tone, and credibility, by the first person. Some themes and meanings require reliability regarding the integrity of character dialogue to have meaningful impact on the reader. So stories improve when authors consider story-specific dialogue that may be different than first-person dialogue.

-A first-person character who is unreliable tends to confuse the reader as to what and who to believe in a story. In character-based fiction, this may work against understanding and accepting the story.

> *We were standing at the edge of the thousand-foot drop on Mount Hood. Carol shivered and looked away from me.*
> *"I'd like to shove your ass into eternity," she said. I smiled.*
> *"I'm not joking," she said.*

In the first-person POV presentation, we do not know what Carol really said, or meant, in the story world; we know only what the first-person POV told us she said. But in a third-person presentation, through a narrator or a character, the recognition of a character through dialogue is sufficiently specific to each character, the story's effectiveness is enhanced.

> *At the precipice, Paul looked down the thousand feet to the snow-covered rocks below. Carol stared at the side of his head, her fists clenched.*
> *"I'd like to shove your ass into eternity," she said. He expected warmth, but her gaze made him unsure what to think. He smiled.*
> *"I'm not joking," she said. The arrogant bastard. She knew exactly what she had to do.*

There are many ways to structure this scene, but the examples show how Carol's words and emotions can be interpreted differently and with more confidence from different POVs. At times, a scene can gain impact when all information is not filtered through the single conduit of the "I" character.

-The first-person POV limits knowing what other characters feel and think—characters who may have a more informed view of the story world and may be better sources of significant conflict and action.

-Because a reader's access is limited to the mind of the "I" character, a reader has no comparative gauge to test credibility of the "I" character's view of the world, accuracy of story presentation, or validity of opinions and conclusions. Credibility in storytelling is a fragile, at times abstract, phenomenon that when highly developed may allow significant impact of story meaning. But when lack of credibility in character, plot, and/or story world perceptions is present, it compromises the effect of a great story purpose.

Using first-person POV

How comfy first-person is for an author! How easy the telling:

> *I was sitting at this gay bar studded with full-size statues of Michelangelo's glorious David at each end, and this girl couple walks in, one ugly, the other so gorgeous she made my heart throb. In a split second, I was falling in love with a dyke, and I hadn't even thrown back a gulp of my straight-up Port Ellen.*

The mood is chatty, with attitude, but the story will be interpreted entirely through a character who provides the reader with only his or her opinions—and thoughts and abilities to observe and articulate the story. The character is inherently unreliable by nature of the first-person POV—can any individual really know and interpret the actual truths that exist around him or her? Indeed, this story type will often rely on the ironies created by what the "I" persona perceives in his/her world.

There are many possible approaches to the use of "I" character. This story could be altered to more in-scene delivery, resulting in seemingly more objective story information and a change of attitude:

> *My heart pounded when I saw a five-foot-two blonde with her girlfriend. She walked with confidence, her short shorts creasing the flesh of her thighs with every step. She smiled and looked away. I gulped my scotch and wondered if she could switch-hit the way I was imagining.*

Moving into the scene, rather than relying on narrative telling, sets a different tone and is more action oriented. The feeling is more objective.

Now compare a delivery from third-person POV (multi-character plus narrator, but should not be thought of as omniscient). Note how information is presented with possible perception in the conscious-ness of multiple characters and the narrator. The different narrative perspective shifts are indicated:

> **Jared sat on a red Naugahyde barstool with his foot on the brass rail, close enough to touch the life-size statue of Michelangelo's *David* that stood at the bar's end as decoration.** (NARRATOR) *He'd wanted Johnnie Walker Black,* (JARED) but the bartender had quotas to meet by serving the most expensive drinks possible, (CHARACTER) **and Jared had wound up with Port Ellen scotch** (NARRATOR) *that didn't do much for his sour mood.* (JARED) **When Doris entered with Camille,** (NARRATOR) <u>their arms linked to express their attachment,</u> (DORIS AND CAMILLE) **Jared's gaze turned to her, and she smiled**, (NARRATOR) <u>not sure if he realized that the obvious desire he couldn't hide would never be satisfied. (DORIS)</u>

Skeptics may reasonably argue that these complexities of point of view are all artificially created, and that authors should do what feels right and is effective for their purpose in their writing— that that is the essence of style. Yet, in literary fiction, the author is trying to intensely engage the reader and provide lasting and significant insights and ideas never before considered. For success, expert characterization and a character-driven plot are necessary, and the more control the author has over the writing and the storytelling, the better the chance to create a lasting, enjoyable, significant story.

Psychic and physical distance in first-person POV

Psychic distance relates to how emotionally involved the character is in the action. It is internal to the character. In terms of psychic distance, the first-person POV limits the breadth of emotional development and restricts one character to a "tight" range of reaction. When story pre-sentation allows character distance, aspects of reasonable and objective information about character, plot, and meaning are enhanced. Psychic distance is more easily created in the third person and with more points of view.

Physical distance is the distance between the character and the action. It is external for the character. Physical distance allows for more expansive imagery and broader interpretations. Different possibilities exist between a first-person POV plunging to almost certain death in airplane seat 24C while telling or showing the pre-death moment and a narrator who describes (even in-scene) after the fact the same disaster by telling or showing the character from a later point in time than depicted in the story, and being able to imagine, and feel, yards or miles or eons away from the action. More objectivity becomes possible, albeit with a loss of immediacy.

Awkward constructions in the first person

The effects of first-person-POV storytelling are distinct from and somewhat more restrictive than other narrative techniques. The first-person POV is often chosen by beginning writers because the style is intuitively easier to execute. Also, as previously mentioned, there is an immediacy and intensity effect, a sort of whisper-in-our-ear phenomenon, that creates intimacy between narrator and reader. That said, the first-person POV has difficulty expressing the feelings of others and relating action that is necessary for the story when the first person cannot be privy to the information or is not present at the event. Compare the following constructions:

> *From the fire in her eyes, I knew exactly how she felt—enraged and hurt, and probably a little embarrassed, too.*

> Her eyes flashed with fire; she cringed with hurt and embarrassment.

> *In the dressing room, I knew the Hardrocks were tuning up, their grimy hands turning the geared pegs, the strings whining with tension.*

> The Hardrocks turned the tuning pegs with grimy hands; the guitar strings whined with tension.

The narrator and the "I" character

ESSENTIALS

-Writing in the first-person POV makes story delivery easier; it is easier to *tell* feelings of love and hate and jealousy than *show* them through action that never uses a specific word that describes the emotion. In literary fiction an author cannot simply recount authorial feelings.   The writing should be character specific for best impact. Action with conflict and resolution objectively presented in the third person is often more effective for creating memorable emotions in the reader.

-First-person POV may seduce an author into making intuitive decisions about story structure that may not be the most appropriate. There must be purpose in how story is told.

-In storytelling, an author creates, a narrator tells, and a character acts. It is usually more prudent not to alter this in first person by collapsing the author into the character to narrate the story. All stories have narrative information that may be awkward or unbelievable when delivered by a first-person character. One solution: a first-person character tells story from an older age with story action at an earlier time, often childhood.

In great stories, the narrator is more knowledgeable about the story world than the character, even in first-person POV. This is one essential ingredient for useful ironies. Many first-person stories simply use the first-person POV to surreptitiously provide narrator information, but this can lead to disbelief and mistrust of the character that in turn leads to a feeling of artificiality in the storytelling. Of course this can be useful if under authorial control. In general, narrators in first person can provide crucial and truthful information and are necessary in almost every first person story.

The same scene with different modes of first-person POV

There was no doubt the ship was sinking. The captain sat alone, stone faced, in his cabin, an illustrious career turned infamous in minutes. In the radio room, the operator had twisted the knob off the now-silent radio and laid his head on his arms. Belowdecks, the engineer failed to seal a compartment door

> *and a rush of water banged his head on a girder, causing him to lose consciousness before he drowned.*
>
> *I watched as the lifeboat hit the water and rocked violently for a few seconds. Someone pushed me from behind. "Dear, God," I muttered. I jumped and felt my lower leg crack as I hit one of the wooden seats that broke my fall.*

Many readers (and writing instructors) would not accept this construction in the first person. A narrator provides information that the first-person-POV character cannot know at the time he delivers this specific information (about the crew, for example). For many readers who find pleasure in serving as POV police, any deviation from a first-person POV is an error, or at least a slippage in writing skills. Below is what might be suggested, or required, in revision. In this example, dialogue is used to deliver story information that can still preserve the first-person POV.

> *We were crowded near the railing on the port side, the deck slanting twenty degrees.*
>
> *"The Captain's taken to his cabin. He ain't seeing no visitors," a man said.*
>
> *"Career ruined," a sailor said.*
>
> *"A dead man," said another.*
>
> *"The radio's out."*
>
> *"Engine room flooded a few minutes ago. I saw the engineer floating face down with my own eyes."*
>
> *Someone pushed me from behind. I looked down to the lifeboat as it hit the water and rocked. A deck officer shoved me. Three of us fell at the same time. My leg cracked as I hit the edge of a wooden seat. Pain seared upward. Someone kicked me in the ribs.*
>
> *"Get out of the way," he said.*

For many, this attempt to provide the story information through dialogue will seem awkward. It rings with a lack of credibility and therefore makes the scene seem less real and harder to accept and enjoy. A major distraction is that the dialogue is delivered as the speakers are facing death, given the chatty-barroom tone (due to exposition mistakenly filtered through dialogue). As an alternative, the information might be provided through first-person internal reflection:

I imagined the captain alone in his cabin, a man with a stellar career ruined. I doubted the distress signals were going out anymore. In fact, the bridge had become silent and eerie compared to the yells and shouts on the deck. A man said the forward compartment had flooded; he thought he heard the cries of the engineer. The lifeboat dropped, the winch handle spinning to a blur. Someone pushed me and I fell, hitting the gunnels. My leg cracked and a searing pain shot upward. Someone kicked me in the ribs to move me out of the way to clear space for others to fall.

This seems awkward, too—strained mainly because of the first-person POV.

With the deck slanting, I could not stand without gripping a rope or a metal ring fixed to the flooring. My fall had broken my leg above the knee; pain seared through me with every movement. But I held on, waiting for the cries to signal when a rescue boat might be below. I was close enough to the rail to be in the crowd who would jump the twenty feet or so below the slanting deck.

"I can't jump," a woman whispered to me, sobbing, clutching my leg to keep from slipping violently into the rail. I yelled out in pain. Was she evil? Did she deserve to die? There was no time to lower her into a boat securely and safely. She'd have to jump. Was there someone to force her? Even with my leg whole, I could never shove a woman, or any human, to possible death. She had to make that decision, not me.

"Do you have family?" I asked. That brought more sobs and she did not answer. The ship's horn blasted. The passengers panicked and began to jump. A few hit the boat, but most went into the water, looking for something to cling to—a deck chair, an oar, some piece of ocean debris. They'd all be unconscious in two to three minutes, motionless with the cold, clumped with broken ice. I began to pray.

This seems better, with the in-scene presentation with the woman in the action.

There is no right way. And when solutions don't readily present themselves, third-person or narrator-dominant presentations are a consideration. But to change a POV is a drastic undertaking: do the information and the scene require first-person POV? If the POV can be easily changed, is it time to delete this scene and use discursive narrative or narrator involvement?

Most authors don't consider alternatives, or narrator-based information, in a first-person-POV-delivered story. They go with a gut feeling of what works, which usually results in the author and character being inseparable. Many of these authors are successful and accepted by readers, and have no need to change if they are satisfied with their work. But ignoring narrator function is not the right attitude for creating a great story. Don't let the ease of writing fictional memoir in the first person—without narrator function considered—hamper the potential of a story.

Present tense and first-person POV

In any presentation (point of view), a story is told from a time point related to the existence of the author and the reader. This can be conceived as the period in which the story is set. Many writers loosely assume that this time is clear when using the first-person POV because the writer creates the story as if it is occurring in the time of the writing.

In truth, all stories have happened. Even futuristic stories have happened in the creator's mind and are being told as if they have occurred. No one reading a story actually lives the story, either at the time the story is created or the time the story is supposed to have happened. At times, present tense is used, especially in first person to create a sense that the story is happening now. This, of course, is a deception—an often acceptable and effective deception–but still not a reality. Verbs indicating present action require suspension of disbelief that the story is happening now.

The pleasing effects of first-person immediacy and strong voice may become tiresome at times, and adding the inherent deception of present tense may work against reader enjoyment of many stories. Still, both present tense and the first person are important tools for every writer.

CHAPTER 9

Desire, Motivations, Emotions

Desire: wanting to have something, or wanting something to happen.

Motivation, motive: the reason someone acts in a certain way.

Desire and motivation are essences of good storytelling, and among the most defining features of literary fiction. In reality, desire and motivation are integral, and dependent on all the other elements of fiction. The desires and motivations of characters may change, and certainly expand in ways that make them seem changed, with story development.

As we look at what desire and motivations can do in a story, we should keep in mind the following principles:

1) In creating scenes, author knowledge of valid character desires allows writing that is maximally effective.

2) For storytelling, core character desires that drive all action are more effective than superficial or poorly considered desires that are questioned, either consciously or subconsciously, by the reader, as significant for motivation.

3) Core desires of characters (and people) are not easily determined.

4) Motivations interact and must be logical for story and character. A change in a motivation expressed in scene, thought, or even backstory will change the effects of other motivations.

ESSENTIALS
-At times, identification and incorporation of desires and motivations in early story drafts is difficult, but as characters develop and action in the plot progresses, incorporation of desire in later drafts and revision

becomes more practical, if not essential, and requires significant revision and restructuring.

-In creating motivations, remember:
    -significance (all-consuming, with serious consequences),
    -credibility (would this character, as developed, really do this?),
    -emotion (action from specific feelings from the character).

-Literary stories are about people, and great stories require in-depth knowledge of the characters' desires and motivations. A character is not a few planks nailed together, floating down with the currents of a river to a calm sea. A character is a carefully crafted one-person sailboat that must tack against the current, catching the right winds, struggling to move upstream against the flow to the river's gushing source. What makes the little sailboat struggle and why? It would be so easy to let the river dictate direction and destination. It is sad that in modern literature, many contemporary stories are simply descriptions of real or imagined events in which characters float through life. Great fictional stories have logical desires and motivations that are embedded in the story drama.

-In memoir or biography, an author describes events that happened and interprets what the perceived desires and motivations of the character were from the actions in the story. In memoir, motivation and desire are discovered in the story being described. In literary fiction, motivation and desire are created and affect the plot. The author can imagine the best desires and motivations of a character and these desires and motivations must be strong, must drive the plot, must be logical and credible (with improvement by multiple revisions), and must heighten the impact of the character's reversal of existing thinking or enlightenment (i.e., theme and meaning).

-Authors must:
    -understand desires and motivations
    -build on desires and motivations with characterization
    -be open to discovery of more effective desires and motivations as the writing progresses,
    -be willing to revise with the most significant desires and motivations in mind.

-assure that desire and motivations relate directly to character change in thinking or enlightenment that creates meaning in a story.

-Delivery of emotions in a story must be paced, and matched to appropriate intensity. Much of this is instinctive for some authors, but when a story is not working, it may be helpful to analyze the rate of delivery of the emotional information, which can improve story momentum and clarity of purpose.

-Hyper-intense emotions tend to narrow the options for a character—that is, available options that are based on a character's action. A character in a murderous rage has narrowed his or her thinking and energy to a precise, concentrated focus. Possible actions are also narrowed and there is, at some point, a need to calm the intensity, which unavoidably slows the action and dampens the emotions.

-Erotic intensity also begins to close down emotional and dramatic options for the writer. With erotic intensity, the character is all-consumingly focused on self, in the satisfaction and attainment of feelings. When eroticism dominates a story, this often closes off the interesting and essential conflicting actions that occur between characters, and which may be necessary for the literary fictional story.

Integrating motives and desires in story creation

-In real life, people react mostly to immediate conflicts and challenges and their short term actions are less driven by inner desires. Fiction is different. Characters, when part of a structured story, require significant, focused reasons for action. And inner core desire, for story consistency, always are involved in character creation. This allows intensity in character development scene after scene, chapter after chapter—development that is cumulative, synergistic, and effective.

-Core desires act as a premise underlying all character motivations in a story and are fewer than might be expected. Examples of good core desires for stories are not easy, but to get the idea, consider, say, fear of eternal damnation as a better desire to work with than guilt over a clandestine sexual experience. An unsatisfied need for adoration provides broader application than an inability to pass by a mirror without looking at oneself. Always seek the core desire that motivates, then develop and revise accordingly.

-Discovering the emotional lines of a successful literary story takes many careful readings. It is useful for learning. In reading a story, and in revising the writing, a four-step process is useful: 1) read the story through without interruption, 2) read it through while making notes on craft and structure, 3) read it through starting with the last few pages, to check for continuity of emotional development, and 4) read it through a last time and trace the emotional relations of each character to determine validity, absence of sentimentality, progression, and significant reasonable change in at least the protagonist.

Emotional complexity

-Emotional complexity, beautifully rendered, perhaps best distinguishes literary fiction from genre fiction. Of course both forms have characters, a dramatic plot, and tension and mystery so the reader keeps reading. But it is the emotional tangles and reversals that occur in the literary story that involve readers and elicit their emotions.

-A character's inner emotions stem from a basic need or want, which is often not obvious until late in the process of story writing. Needs come from inner turmoil. And turmoil has two sides.

> Examples of contrasting emotions:

> > bad / good
> > hate / love
> > forgiveness / revenge

-If a character feels abandoned, he or she may repress it with a contrasting, overly friendly behavior, or with sullen inaction. If a character feels unjustly accused, it may be expressed via opposing emotions such as anger, or timidity, or spite. Finding these interactions is essential for building emotional complexities through the craft of prose, and for developing power in the story momentum and interest.

-Emotions are almost never as effective when described in narrative as when they are illuminated for the reader through action. Action takes more story time to express and is harder to write, but it has less inclination toward sentimentality and is more easily accepted as credible and true by the reader.

He loved Peggy.

Love is a general and abstract (as opposed to specific and concrete) term that tells nothing specific about the man's love for Peggy. The narrator is telling how the character feels.

Before sleep, his eyes closed, the image of Peggy haunted him: her mysterious smile and magnetic blue eyes, misty yet so distant. He knew his desire to touch her was impossible, and she faded away.

This is overwritten and trite, but the feeling for Peggy is still better established in the longer, more concrete passage. The narrator is showing how the character feels. Showing emotions can happen in the dramatic present of a scene, and does not have to be in the character's consciousness.

-The concept of transferring emotions to the reader, as opposed to telling the reader about a character's emotions, is not easy to explain or grasp. On a simplistic level, compare: *"She was so sad,"* to *"She wept, her body trembling."* One is telling, one is showing. Another example: *"Go jump in the lake,' he said angrily,"* to *"He grabbed her by the ankles and held her over the cliff until she pleaded for mercy."* While admittedly overly obvious for good writing, the second lines use action to show emotion, rather than telling the reader how the character feels.

Sentimentality

Sentimentality is almost totally subjective. Sentimental emotions will be rejected by a reader when the emotions have not been earned through action and credible character development. Writer should not use clichés or hackneyed descriptions, or simply extraneous authorial ideas, to get an abstract idea across to the reader.

Literary writers seek to satisfy the sentimental aesthetics and acceptance of a specific reader, usually a reader seeking enjoyment from perfectly crafted stories as an art form. Stories should be without cliché, with primarily action scenes, and credibly unique characters. It is a failure when a writer cannot convince a specific reader through the quality of the prose that an emotion is real.

In genre fiction, sentimentality sells. Plots are repetitive, characters stereotyped, outcomes predictable—all outcomes of openly sentimental writing. Romance readers, in fact, seek sentimentality and, as proof of its popularity, romance genre fiction sells far more successfully than literary fiction.

Heroes

A touch of hero is in almost every great character of classic literature. In the story world, heroes exude qualities such as persistence, morality, perseverance, determination, strength, confidence, intellect, and/ or unfailing expectations that things are going to turn out all right.

Hero characters, in fiction, show resistance to the status quo, often in the face of insurmountable odds or conflicts in which the character must use skills, and even develop additional skills, in order to succeed. Success and failure, of course, will vary from story to story but it's the struggle and the authorial delivery that grab the reader. Readers generally want to root for a character who succeeds by using imagination and hard work. If the author of fiction writes to evoke reader sympathy without significant reader engagement, there can be unwanted consequences. Sympathy comes from empathy for the plight of others.

Victims as characters in literary fiction

A described victim is a sufferer, the injured party, prey. Born victims are losers, patsies, suckers, fools. But these traits are subjective, as well as the idea of who is a victim and who is not.

A reader should agree that the victim has been injured or wronged unjustly. Authors in control of their storytelling write to create specific responses in their targeted readers. Knowing the character and controlling the story for the reader's response can accomplish this.

A victim's self-perception is important. A victim is easily absorbed by injustice, causing inaction. This inaction prohibits the character from redefining themselves and their life situation, and results in self-sympathy and self-pity. Thus, attention to how the victim perceives their misfortune directs either 1) an active response to improve one's state, or 2) a passive submission to life's challenges. Active responses work better in literary fiction.

As readers, we have been moved for centuries by characters striving for change and not succumbing to victimization as an excuse for inaction: Jane Eyre, Elizabeth Bennett, Anna Karenina, Heathcliff, Milly Theale (*The Wings of the Dove*), Emma Bovary, Captain Ahab, Charles Marlow (*Heart of Darkness*), Scrooge, Cinderella, and even Flaubert's Felicité.

Consider, as a writer, these goals when creating characters as victims: 1) stay objective, 2) don't succumb to converting a reader to your assessment of injustice in victimization, 3) make your characters unique, incapable of clichéd thinking and response with regard to victimization, and 4) avoid predetermination of the validity of the injustice. Let the reader determine her or his opinion from the storytelling.

Summary

In literary fiction, emotions of characters must be complex; must be carried through a story with an arc-like, intense change; must not be sentimental; and must be logical for the story plot and characterization. Writing a great literary story depends on different emphases and requirements of emotional complexity. Writers need skill in creating prose that works effectively so they can incorporate thinking about emotional complexities in their story creations.

CHAPTER 10

Time

No other storytelling medium comes close to what prose fiction can accomplish, and no other medium of expression is as hard to master and use successfully.

It is awkward to write about real time in constricted story time. Stories are about the past, and of necessity, they are condensed to be read in a minute fraction of what the story would cover if lived in real time. Writers either consciously or intuitively construct a story timeline. When does the story start, and how long does it take to end in story time? Hours, weeks, years, millennia?

All story events are placed on the story timeline, and the storytelling gives the illusion that they are happening in real time. Writers use various techniques to adhere to, and orient the reader to, a story timeline: transitions, flashbacks, writing in scene, moving characters in seconds of story time through actions that would take hours or days of real time, and careful adjustment of pacing of action and prose.

For a writer, a clear conception of the timeline allows clarity of writing, appropriateness of voice, acceptable pacing, effective transitions, and logic and credibility of the story illusion.

Real time versus story time

Real time is what every human lives. Story time is the time a reader spends with the story from beginning to end. It can be a few minutes, many hours, or even days. Time is a human invention, and not necessarily a divine truth. Humans live and die. Time is how we orient our existence; living takes so many minutes and is defined by humanity's perception of the physical world. Who knows whether, outside human meaning, collective consciousness, and experience, time has meaning? Writers, who create in real time, have to learn to adjust writing, structuring, pacing, and story conceptualization to create a credible story in illusion, where time is compressed but must seem like real time.

Quality of story illusion

For story writers, the written word creates an imagined world and series of events in the mind of a reader. No direct visual or auditory sensations are possible. Readers must translate from abstract letters on the page into images, feelings and complex thoughts. A writer's skill is dependent entirely on the interpretation of the written language delivered.

A great literary fictional story is received as credible. To be meaningful, two crucial accomplishments are necessary: 1) the reader understands and accepts the illusion as it is presented (and the story takes on special impact), and 2) the reader subconsciously follows a progressive, condensed timeline that is delivered in a minute fraction of real time, but is convinced that the characters living the story did so in real time.

Voice, time and presentism

All stories are written about the past, whether it is a matter of a few hours or a near-eternity. As time progresses, the world changes physically, and a writer's interpretation of the world changes in perception, opinion, interpretations, cultural characteristics, and especially linguistics. Writers—and sometimes narrators—tell stories from a vastly different world than the story world. When the present world of the writer (or narrator) seeps into the story world, the story weakens.

Time has a considerable effect on voice in fiction. *Voice* is everything a character says, and is affected by all the character thinks and feels (unique to prose), and says. In any story, many voices may be present: characters, narrator, and (rarely) even the author. And strong credible character/narrator specific voices make for better quality storytelling. Each voice is limited to characteristics consistent with the story world's "reality".

Story time is always earlier than the time the story was written and features of life and the world the exists after the setting of story time is created are not infused into story. In other words, a voice in a story cannot consist of features from what would be from the story world's future or another character's, or human's, world.

Presentism is the use of information from when the story is created in a story that is happening the past. Presentism can result in a loss of credibility and authenticity in voice, and confuse the timeline of the story.

This may seem to be only important in historical fiction, but for great literary fiction, it is also a crucial consideration. Readers intuitively know when voice errors disrupt a story—whether the error stems from faulty conceptualization, construction, or adherence to the timeline—and will reject the story for that reason.

A writer can only create from his or her perception of a reality that is, by necessity of existing, changing. How the writer sees and feels about humanity, objects, and events changes. Ideation of imagery and persuasion changes, and linguistics are constantly evolving. Relentlessly, the present becomes history. The story written by the author must stay true to the setting, culture, intellect, and memories of people in the story world.

In **summary,** there can be no carrying of the author's real-world imagery, voices, ideation, or beliefs into the past of the story world. That story world has its own distinct relation to human interaction and development based on the timeline, and where that timeline is in the spectrum of our human existence.

Mismanagement of the timeline through presentism, uneven pacing, voice aberrations from the future, or inconsistent dialogue will undermine the illusion that is a literary story. For the writer to maintain the story illusion, management of time, internal logic, and credibility are crucial. The story is like a soap bubble, vulnerable to the slightest assault.

CHAPTER 11

Second-Person Narration

More than a few editors see stories with second-person narration as trendy:

> *You enter the church; you kneel at the altar. You stare into the downcast eyes of the statue of the Virgin and wonder if she's listening.*

Some readers accept this without question as compelling, innovative writing. Others find it irritating. Rob Spillman, editor of *Tin House,* has gone on record: "I have a pet peeve against the second person that I call the second-person accusatory: 'You are walking down the street.' I go, 'No, I am not walking down the street!'"[1]

Spillman is not the only one who feels this way. The second-person POV constantly confronts the reader, assuming he or she will react positively, and will be drawn into the story, but it requires greatly increased suspension of disbelief (regarding narrator credibility and accuracy) for the reader to actually enjoy the story.

David Lynn, editor of the *Kenyon Review,* who admits to a general distaste to second-person-narration, offers the following critique of a short story written in the second person by a writer he liked and published.

> 1) Second-person narrative successfully emphasizes author lack of being a full, mature "subject" capable of first-person story making.
> 2) The "you" sets the author/narrator apart as an object, not in control of his own narrative.

---

1 http://www.storyinliteraryfiction.com/interviews/spillman-rob-interview/

3) Mere clumsiness or lack of authorial skill may be perfectly appropriate to the narrator and the situation.
4) Awkwardness and confusion of the language, heightening nightmarish qualities.
5) Author marvelously skilled at suggesting and representing the challenges of multiple languages and failures of understanding, without being heavy handed.[2]

In the creation of literary fiction stories (the story Lynn refers to seems to be a memory-based "fictional" story), a number of essentials need to be considered to reach memorability and acceptance as great writing and storytelling: clarity of the prose narration, solid imagery that stimulates and engages the reader's imagination, clear ideation, unique and sophisticated character development with some reversal of thought and understanding, theme, meaning, and the provision of entertainment and enlightenment for the reader.

In second-person narration, there is a barrier set between the author and the reader. When "you" is used instead of a first-person or third-person pronoun, there is little accumulation of valid character-ization because the "you" is unanchored in an identifiable narrator. The reader becomes dependent mostly on narrative description, since internalization, action, and dialogue are now attributed to a hazy, unidentifiable story presenter. And it is often unclear whether the author means "you" as a singular entity or a plural one, which would suggest an even more diffuse identification of who the story presenter is, and more than a little authorial arrogance in believing that all the world will believe as he or she does.

Second-person use results in a lack of narrator control over the story. For great fictional stories, a strong, identifiable narrator presence in control of the storytelling is almost always an advantage. This issue of an unclear narrator eroding characterization is best shown by example:

> *You are insecure about Helen's meaning. You see her raised eyebrow as questioning your authority, so you pull the trigger. You are pleased at the puzzlement in her last look.*

---

2 David Lynn, "Why We Chose It" *Kenyon Review* September 11, 2012

Almost surely the reader won't relate to this pronoun and accept responsibility for the "you's" thoughts and actions. And if the reader does accept the convention of "you," the characters inevitably fail to take on form and personality; the reader is left floating in a confused, awkward, not-quite-knowing the characters involved. Now let's try the first person:

> I'm not sure what Helen means. But her innocent look inflames me and I pull the trigger, happy to see the surprise in her eyes as the life goes out of her.

And now the third person:

> He does not know Helen's meaning. He is incapable of under-standing a soul so trusting and pure. He takes her pleading gaze as mockery and pulls the trigger; he smiles at her stare of surprise and disbelief as she dies.

In both the first and the third person, action and thoughts allow the reader to know characters—a feat essential for good fiction.

In these variations using first-, second-, and third-person narration, the second person does not allow any assumptions as to how the narrator felt or why he or she acted. Both the first and the third person support the storytelling better.

Summary

When writers who write to please readers use the second person, they risk alienating the reader, confusing the reader, failing to develop strong characters, and clouding motivations, desires, and cause and effect in the telling of the story. The trend continues, and academic teachers sometimes even encourage the second-person form. Writers will have to make a decision based on their personal goals for telling fictional prose stories. For writers who aspire to create quality literary fiction that persists in the consciousness of readers, second-person narration may not be a dependable tool.

CHAPTER 12

Why Literary Stories Fail

In literary fiction, the author creates, through imagination, a story that causes some enlightenment or change in thinking about the human condition. If the author is successful, the story is unforgettable. The reader's enjoyment comes from sympathizing with the character(s), sometimes without even liking them, and finding satisfaction in realizing how character traits drive the plot progression.

For the serious writer, literary fiction is not memoir, nor creative nonfiction, nor dependent on autobiographical material, although these techniques are commonly used and accepted in what is commonly called nongenre, or mainstream, fiction. But devoted writers find literary fiction difficult to craft but representative of high achievement. And when the characterization and the plot depend more on reality of self than on the imagination, the writer loses an artistic edge of excellence.

Literary fictional stories fail for a number of reasons:

-Failure to engage the reader

The success of a literary story requires engagement on the part of the reader with both the story action and the protagonist. The reader wants to experience what the character experiences, and must sympathize with the character as early as possible in the story's development.

-Overly clever prose

A great literary story describes a series of events full of conflict and action that result in meaningful resolution through enlightenment or change in existing thought. The author achieves this through accurate word choice; logical thought progression; concrete, fresh imagery; and perfectly chosen metaphoric enlightenments. Never is a story improved when accuracy, logic, freshness, or effective metaphors are compromised by the author slipping into a mode in which cleverness resulting in lyricism, abstract ideas, unclear word choice becomes more important than the story. Certainly some readers seek out and enjoy expansive prose, and lyrical prose can be beautifully clear, image-filled, and significant. But inflated, expanded, baroque prose undermines succinct, purposeful story writing. In great literary stories, there is little space for showcasing an author's love for his or her skills in manipulating the language. In great literary storytelling, the words are like notes whose pitch and positioning produces a melody that evokes a human effect, and the quality of the effect is consistent, whether it is presented by a symphony, a rap star, a jazz combo, or a monastic modal organ recital. Great words well chosen and in alignment form a melodic impression that is remembered.

It is that core melodic value we seek in writing, and the tendency to overdo, or sublimate, the presentation of that melody erodes the value of the fiction. Cleverness is, of course, subjective, but readers will recognize when clever prose becomes irritating and stop reading, or at least lose concentration.

-Excessive and/or static details

Setting is essential for story. Excessive description of setting is not. And when description is excessive, it is almost always static. For clarification of "static," compare the examples below.

> *The small black bird with the brilliant red wings and inquisitive yellow eyes perched on the white picket fence just out of reach of the tabby-colored cat with a scar on his leg, one eye half-closed and scarred from some long-ago fight.*

> *The red-winged blackbird glided in for a landing. The battle-tested tabby cat leaped up, claws out, and caught only the edge of wings to scratch a feather loose. The feather floated down to the garden path and the bird landed safely on the fence a few feet away.*

Too many adjectives, adverbs, or extended, vague metaphorical comparisons can deaden the desired effect of a story telling, and should be avoided in favor of action verbs and nouns that provoke mental images.

-In-your-face attitude

When characterization and plot motivation fail to produce meaning and effect, writers lean on voice and character attitude to try to save the story. The writing filters the characters' thinking and speech through an in-your-face, often counter to existing convention, attitude, and through authoritative, confrontational, usually descriptive narrative. Even when done well, the effect is limited. In literary fiction stories, characterization develops when deep character traits are dependent for credibility on actions, responses to events, and in-scene development. In-your-face narrative tends to be most useful in a character sketch, and rarely useful to develop a character who acts with strong, credible motivations to drive the plot in significant ways.

-Fatalism

Fatalism is plot predictability. Predictability is what a reader of genre fiction expects. Murder, investigation, justice. Man woos reluctant woman, they fall in love. Terrorist threatens the White House, terrorist thwarted. In literary fiction, plots are character driven—that is, the action results from the free-will decisions of the major characters. Rather than ferreting out a murderer, a reader learns motivations and desires (the how and why), and these must be understandable and credible (the hard part). Life may seem—and could be—predestined and fatalistic. Literary fiction, however, moves ahead on the foundation of human foibles, and is exciting and unpredictable—never predestined.

-Need to shock

Too many failing stories resort to shock to keep the reader entertained. Horror films shock in order to delight those who enjoy shock. But in literary fiction, producing a shocking action, or reveling in visually uncomfortable detail, doesn't produce effective character development or meaningful, character-driven plots. Even if shock creates an effect in a literary story, it cannot be the major element of an effective story construction. Innovation, surprise, and uniqueness are all elements of good writing, but in literary fiction, stretching for shock by detailed description of an alien-like animal devouring a human intestine ultimately detracts from the creation of a great story.

-Insignificance

Great literary stories are written with purpose. They say something, and they say it well. Fiction is the best way to achieve this. It allows story development unhindered by descriptions of a set reality, and provides unlimited choices in character motivations and actions that support the purpose and momentum of the story. Significance is not achieved when the fiction is loosely conceived.

The author's conscious will must be in control of the story creation. It cannot simply let ideas bubble up from the unconscious, or discover them in the description of a life experience where the significance is tagged on late in the writing, like a stamp on a letter. Significance emerges from planned stories in which characters change to a new way of thinking and understanding (enlightenment about the human condition).

Significance is often directly related to an emotional experience for a reader. Reader emotions vary from story to story in intensity and type (joy, fear, sympathy, love, anger, et cetera). Emotions are best evoked by total engagement in a fictional dream that requires the inclusion of the reader in the story rather than simply treating the reader as a listener or voyeur. This means showing why and how in scene or dramatic narrative, and not simply describing real or imagined events or thoughts.

A story will never be significant if a reader finishes and has no understanding of why it was written, and can't remember characters or what the story was about. A writer must master not only the craft of creating interesting dramatic prose, but also the entangled process of purposeful storytelling.

BOOK TWO

Creating a Literary Fictional Story

Stories are told for many reasons: information, pride, teaching, rendering, warning, entertainment, intimidation. In its basic form, a story starts, happens, and ends, but literary stories provide opportunities for in-depth characterization, with desires and motives that integrally relate to plot movement. Characters in literary fiction must be carefully constructed for story purpose, and engage in memorable, in-scene action. They are involved in dramatic plots, and they are capable of enlightened change, for better or for worse.

CHAPTER 1

Fundamentals of Telling a Literary Story

Consider these eight elements as you review your writing process:

Prose relates to diction, syntax, and voice. Lyric prose with intensely poetic elements can be used to pleasing effect for a reader as a secondary element and even as a primary one, but in general, attention to clarity, accuracy, and the concrete over the abstract are conducive to the most effective prose for significant storytelling.

Characterization is a key element for a literary story and is often most effective when in-scene action predominates over discursive, narrative telling. Characterization is important in story development, and in great stories it is unique and individual, and requires talent and practice. Dialogue, narrative, internalization, flashback, diction, memory, and voice are opportunities for character development and can be different, and at times superior, to characterizations in film or the theater. Almost without exception, great character-based stories integrate characterization and plot progression. Each primary character has a recognizable core desire that contributes to solid logic of character motivations and reactions.

Plot is all that happens in a story. For great stories, the plot is almost always: structured with a beginning, middle, and end; character-based; dependent for momentum on reversals and recognition, mystery and suspense; primarily linear; and interwoven with emotional, character, and story arcs. Great plots provide conflicts early, both in the story's action and among characters.

Narration is storytelling. Characters act in fiction stories, the narrator tells the story, and the author creates the story with imagination and uniqueness. The selection of a point of view is tailored to the needs of story. Most readers prefer distinct, even authoritative, voices for the narrator and characters in fiction as an art form. Different points of view have advantages and disadvantages and must conform to reasonable requirements regarding credibility, reliability, and suspension of disbelief. Narrative perspective is not just about POV; it is integral to voice and credibility. Authorial control of the narration through the narrator and characters must be consistent, complete, and meticulous.

Setting orients the reader to time, place, and their physical and psychic distance from story action, environment, and obstacles to plot progression. Most great literary stories provide setting detail through subtle integration with other elements, avoiding extensive, uninterrupted description.

Imagery relies on imaginative prose with innovative yet accurate word choice within the boundaries set up by story development. Image-inducing prose should have pervasive, inherent movement whenever possible to keep the reader engaged.

Meaning and purpose are crucial. Every story should engage the reader, entertain the reader, please the reader, and provide recognition or enlightenment (i.e., meaning) so the reader will never again see the world exactly as it seemed before the story was read. Great fiction stories are not character sketches, memoirs, biographies, or journalism imbued with untruths; they are imagined. Great stories are *about* something—they have themes of love or hate or revenge. Every great story has to be more than an authorial catharsis describing real events and real characters with remembered imagery and actions and discursive rumination.

Drama maintains the reader's interest, moves the plot, and builds character. Drama is conflict that precipitates action that results in resolution, and it requires a writer's ability to insert action in scene, in dialogue, and in narrative description. Drama also can move the reader to feel involvement in the story and attachment to the characters.

Characterization, and how characters come alive

Characters populate stories and are developed through the accumulation of carefully chosen facts and actions that stimulate the reader's imagination to fill in gaps of characterization not directly provided. A delicate balance is required in order to provide enough information to allow the reader to know the character and plot details, yet leave enough room for the reader to add his or her own imaginative details. Writers must leave space in the story if readers are to become actively involved.

Every character in literary fiction, as with all interesting humans, must have a serious desire—a desire that underlies his or her motivations. These desires might never be directly stated, but they must be clear to the reader and related to the movement and theme of the story.

Characters' desires and needs motivate action and change. With story development, careful narrowing (and concentrating) of the characters' desires strengthens the logic and reader acceptance of what happens in the story.

The true core desire of a character is usually discovered as the plot solidifies and layers of characterization are created. The first desires recognized are rarely the most useful, since essential characteristics are not yet fully present in the prose. Careful, repeated revision embeds core desires of characters into all elements of the story.

Authors often structure a story so that readers ponder mysteries and encounter surprise. Ironically, an unanticipated surprise is best when readers feel they knew it was coming.

Readers must be guided to make their own discoveries and should not be manipulated, misdirected, or forced into reactions to story or character. All of this is achieved by believable, in-depth characterization and meticulous logic in the cause and effect of plot development. It is this difficult-to-achieve edge that makes the literary fictional story so special—and so difficult to write.

Based on their life experiences, readers subconsciously begin to group characters in knowable boxes—good or bad, likable or unlikable, smart or dumb, moral or immoral, or just like so-and-so. Without sufficient in-depth creative characterization, readers will pigeonhole characters into stereotypical clichés that are ineffective or inappropriate for literary fiction.

Internal reflection and interiorization

Internal reflection is a powerful storytelling technique; it lets the reader know what a character thinks and feels. But writers tend to overuse it at the expense of character action, primarily when the writer defaults to descriptive writing from memory rather than the creation of story and plot to provide maximum engagement, entertainment, and enlightenment. Writers who are inattentive to technique expound on things tangential or unrelated to story movement and theme. Great literary stories are not essays and rarely memoirs.

Interiorization refers to an author making an idea or a thought a valuable a part of the character's inner self or mental structure. It is related to enlightenment and epiphany in literature. A character always starts out with unlimited options regarding things to do and say. But as the story progresses and the character develops, these options narrow. As a character evolves, the persona begins to provide credible options to the writer. Readers do not think in terms of decreasing options for a character, but they will be disturbed if the character does or says something that isn't what would be reasonably expected at that specific point in the story's development. If inappropriate character responses happen too often, the reader rejects the character and the story. Readers want to have solid reasons to believe in characters.

By the end of the story, the characters should be so well formed, so deeply ingrained, that the important late happenings—so crucial for meaning—have influenced the reader to accept character actions and dialogue consistent with their developed personas.

Feelings and emotions

Expression of character emotion is a key skill for the writer. Errors or apathy in describing feelings may lead to sentimentality, or, at worst, rejection of the story.

Feelings in a story can be told. "He was angry with her." Although necessary at times, this lacks energy and taxes reader interest. ("Angry" is abstract.) Although it is much more strenuous to write and takes up more story time, authors can show feeling far more effectively through action and dialogue: "'You are the worst, most degenerate liar I've ever known,' he shouted." This shows anger ("shouted") and hints at a morality issue via concrete words such as "degenerate" and "liar."

Feelings must be consistent to the character and the moment. Even slight inappropriateness will erode the reader's trust. Every author must develop his or her own sensibilities about when feelings assist the story. In literary fiction, authorial management of emotion must be part of the writer's style. This is not just "varnish"; conflicted feelings, well presented, are the essence of good literary-quality writing.

PRINCIPLES for characterization

-Characters are developed by action and reaction, dialogue, internal reflection, internalization, rhetorical questions, emotions, diction (choice of words and context), narrative, exposition, integration with setting and description of scene, the author's familiarity with the character's story line, and backstory.

-Desires must be internally powerful in order to force unavoidable and credible actions.

-Actions should convey character emotion for maximum effect at appropriate times.

-Throughout the story, characterization must be continuously and seamlessly layered, true to story and character, interesting, and dynamic.

-Characters must be in conflict with someone or something (sometimes themselves).

-As the character becomes stronger to the reader through detail and familiarity, the character's options for action and dialogue become fewer and carry more significance, which is the maturation of characterization.

-Excellent characterization provides strong motivations of characters as the story progresses.

-Expressing character emotions through action is better than simply naming the emotion. Rather than "She was in love," show what characters in love do: they have funny sensations in their chests, they ache when separated, they have an irrepressible desire to be closer, always closer. Work to find concrete, fresh ideas that are right for the story and will engage readers.

GUIDELINES for characterization

-Show the character's desires, don't tell the desires, although the latter is easier.

-Don't doom characters to a preordained fate; they must have possibilities to choose.

-As you write a story, don't forget important characters introduced earlier. Never lose characters that are important to story development and outcome.

-Although it is essential to use the point of view of a character or a narrator, remember that too much access to one character's point of view can be deadening. This simple rule makes first-person narration more difficult to use successfully.

-A character from life that is described with adherence to reality is limited in the dynamic, unique, fictional character development necessary in the best literary fiction. Don't let a favorite real-life character description or favorite author-involved real event obfuscate imaginative characterization when creating story drama, interest, suspense, and story individuality.

-Check character development by studying a unified overview of all actions and dialogue of the character in the story. Be sure that words and actions are driven by motivations that are right for the time in the character's story development and are reasonable for the exact moment in the story. This is one of the most difficult skills to develop as a fiction writer, but it is key to excellence and developing an admired, unique identity for an author.

-Beware of inappropriate responses in dialogue among multiple characters, especially with respect to words, syntax, and ideation. Each character's response must fit the immediate range of emotions of that character, and all the characters, at that story moment. When character responses are specific to individual personalities and chosen for reader enjoyment, the basic momentum of the story, as well as readers' acceptance of it, are enhanced.

-For most effective expression of feelings, avoid abstract words such as "love," "anger," "pity," or "hate," and instead express ideas through actions, dialogue, and thoughts.

Plotting

In general, plot is everything that happens in the story related to action, momentum, and change. But in literary fiction, characterization is usually a main element of plot; it is the inner story of characters that contributes to the outer story of plot action. It is easy to discuss but difficult to execute, mainly because making the character's inner story believable, unique, and forceful takes skill and practice so that it integrates seamlessly with the plot. Simply telling your life story, sufficiently altered to be accepted as fiction, will rarely if ever suffice if the desire is to create imaginative literary fiction with dynamic original characters.

Common plot types in genre fiction (for example search, revenge, rivalry, quest, or mystery) rarely require development of characters to the emotional level needed in literary stories. This makes literary stories unique: the characters' thoughts, emotions, and actions generate the plot. In action-reaction genre plots, characters often act without regard to inner conflicts, and the stories are fatalistic and dependent on coincidence or conflicts void of emotional character maturation.

Plot structure

The **beginning** is the point in a story from which everything follows. Failure to adhere to this major concept is a common misstep. Don't leap back in time to the past to start a story unless it relates to the bulk of the story's present in some insightful way. Strive for unity that doesn't jerk the reader back and forth in story time. And don't succumb to using backstory for extraneous ideas for characterization narrative if they could be worked unobtrusively into the story's present.

ESSENTIALS
- The first sentence must be interesting.
- Introduce major characters first, or early.
- Begin with as much revelation as possible with respect to where the story is going; readers need a sense of their destination.
- In general: never start with a flashback, never start with the past perfect tense ("he had plastered himself and his motorcycle against a brick wall") and never start with a negation ("Billie could never climb as well as Susie, even though he was older.")

- Dialogue essential to the reader can provide effective characterization, but does not easily set the place, tone, and direction. Avoid dialogue as a start to a story.

The **middle** is the arc of the story—where the story moves and the characters evolve. It is essential to stay on track:

ESSENTIALS
- Avoid temptations to wander and slip in ideas that are unimportant to the story.
- Keep character emotions and action-progression smooth and logical.
- Keep looking for the theme.
- Don't use extraneous detail unrelated to the story.
- Don't fall into excessive discursive narrative description when story momentum lags. Consider dialogue, internalization, and in-scene action to maintain momentum and reader interest.
- Stay in the scene wherever possible to maintain drama and a sense of movement.

The **ending** is the point in the story after which nothing else of story significance happens.

ESSENTIALS
- Endings should have elements of surprise, yet must not be *too* surprising. An ending should be reasonable, yet not predictable. An ending should not be too devastating nor too redemptive, but should demonstrate some recognizable—and memorable—change in one or more major characters.
- Stories must not fall apart at the end; an author should direct the reader's feelings, not demand them.
- Readers should discover something new and unique. For maximum impact, endings should *show* emotional and intellectual awakenings and reversals, not *tell* them.
- Resolutions must be clear in order to satisfy the reader, they must be directly tied to the conflict, and they must be a result of previous actions.
- Avoid trying to evoke emotion in a reader by telling a character's state of mind through clichés and sentimental images; the drama and action should provide the reader with a meaningful emotional response.

An example of an ineffective ending (due to clichés and sentimentality):

With a heavy heart, he sat on the carcass of his dead horse, the weight of the world light compared to his grief—a grief that would only grow with time. True friendships can never be replaced.

Interaction of emotion and plot progression

The plot line is integrated with and dependent on good characterization in literary fiction. It represents the emotional flow of the characters and generates and explains motives. All inner thoughts and emotions should be reasonable to the character's life, education, and intelligence. Errors will reduce the emotional impact and believability of the character.

The outer story is dependent on conflict, action, and resolution. It should be logical and have clear evidence of cause and effect. Careful choice of in-scene or narrative telling with imagined interdependent scenes is crucial.

Transitions

The art of transition is essential to good storytelling. In a film, the story goes from scene to scene and the visual orientation to time of day and place is usually immediate. In literary fiction, unless readers are aware from previous content, they must be oriented via transitions to a new scene's physical environment—who, what, when, where—and to shifts in emotion and perceptions. At every level of story presentation, transitions lead the reader from one time to another, from place to place, among points of view and changes in thought, from idea to idea and emotion to emotion.

-Line spaces in formatting (and/or markings for section or chapter breaks) are often used for transitions, but these breaks should be carefully chosen and should not replace a well-written transition that will enhance the story and the reader's understanding.

-Be sure the reader will comprehend the reason for the transition, time shift, setting change, character changes, POV shift, et cetera. Do not try to create suspense by using personal pronouns in transitions—"he," "she," or "they"—that confuse the reader because there is not a clear and juxtaposed antecedent. Use "John drove…" rather than "He drove…" whenever it is appropriate, and avoid ambiguities such as: "He served the spaghetti to him but he didn't respond until he spoke, his face red with anger."

Transitions usually condense action or description; be careful to include only the most important information in the transition. Transitions should be succinct.

Outline

An outline is a prioritized list of main-point story elements that organizes scenes; establishes timelines; tracks characters; embeds emotional arcs and conflicts; and includes whatever else may improve a story by logical, credible (for the story), and dramatic presentation. While outlines may be entirely a mental process, a written one can be a valuable tool. Keep in mind:

PRINCIPLES

- Stories are constructions of elements working together synergistically.

- Structure makes these various elements maximally effective.

- An outline can help identify meanings and theme before the writing process begins.

- Outlines are processes (of story creation) and not end products (a final draft).

GUIDELINES

-Test yourself: Can you tell a summary of your story verbally, without notes, in a manner that holds a listener's interest?

-What is the major conflict of the story? (In a novel there may be many.) What is the action precipitated by this conflict, and what is the resolution of the conflict? Are you clear about what the resolution is (even if you expect it to change as part of the necessary creative process as the story develops—a creative ingredient of imagination not nurtured in nonfiction)?

-Do you know before you begin writing when and why your story will start, how it will end, and all that will happen in between (to create engagement, suspense, mystery, enlightenment, significance, and entertainment)?

CHAPTER 2

Essentials of Literary Story Writing

Narration

Narration—the telling of a story—is the storyteller's technique of entertaining, engaging, and enlightening a reader. In literature, the intended reader is seeking creativity expressed in readable, admirable prose, with the author showing control and purpose. Various points of view (POVs) are possible: first person, second person, third person, and multiple (frequently referred to as omniscient, although this is incorrect). In fiction, the sophisticated use of a narrator is almost always an advantage, and great authors often use a strong narrator presence. Voices of the characters and the narrator are most effectively created from characters and narrators using author-created world-views, intellect, education, memory, and humor. Authors of literature should not default and use their own worldview, intellect, education, memory, and humor—a mistake that suppresses those seeking the broadest understanding of the world and human existence.

Certain POVs have different uses. In the first-person POV, there are limitations of story information through one intellect, one voice, and a single worldview that can strain credibility, threaten the suspension of disbelief that all fiction requires, and make questionable the reliability of theme and meaning. Make POV and narrative choices that allow the characters some flexibility in actions, changes in thinking and beliefs, and open to reversals and discoveries. Don't box characters into stereotypical responses by errors in POV choice and ineffective narrative perspective.

GUIDELINES
Test yourself: Have you established POV(s) and narrative perspective(s) for your story, and is it consistent?

Does your choice of POV and development of character voice build a unique character with special characteristics and qualities? Characterization is the lifeblood of the literary fictional story!

Is your story dynamic and filled with subjective plotting and changing action, while simultaneously objective and reader-friendly in its delivery?

Drama = Conflict + action + resolution

Scenes are the dramatic units that make up a story. As sentences are to paragraphs, scenes are to stories: scenes are the building blocks that contribute to the theme and action of the entire story. As with characterization, conflict, clarity of prose, credibility, and reliability are essential to scenes and plot.

Conflict is the basis of the majority of scenes. Every moment of our lives, we are in conflict with the environment, other living creatures, society, imagination, and sometimes even with our own decisions, thoughts, and emotions.

Conflicts may be physical, emotional, mental, or verbal. They can be multiple or single, simple or complex; they may pit a person against another person, or against a family, self, reality, friend, enemy, environment, values, morality, lust, or authority.

In literary fiction, conflict is often developed between two or three (or more) characters. Special skills are required for a single-character scene to provide deep and intense conflict sufficient for the reader to become involved.

A character may be confronted with nonhuman conflict by obstacles to obtaining desires, or threats to success or survival. Conflict precipitates action and is most effective when under the author's imaginative control. Quality development of character personalities helps readers respect and sympathize with characters, both good and bad. Action with conflict is best shown in-scene with narrative summary used for brevity, condensed action, and transitions. And drama is an essence of literary fiction of quality.

Resolution of scene action tells the reader how the character, or the situation, was changed by the action. Resolution is the calmer sea after the violence of a storm—the meaningful reflections after emotional or intellectual chaos—and a chance for reflection and understanding by the reader.

In-scene and narrative telling of conflicts

In-scene development captures the reader's interest and is often the best choice for story delivery that provides maximum enjoyment. Yet it requires more time to write and more space on the page. Thus, narrative telling of scene conflict is useful in transitions and when time for in-scene development does not allow for smooth, forward progress of the story. Most great stories have more in-scene development than narrative telling. Discursive prose that is not story related should be avoided. Consider:

> *The ship sank.*

Versus:

> *Through the cloud of mist and smoke, he saw the ocean liner list, taking on water through the hole the torpedo made in the portside. The bridge shuddered from two explosions in the engine room, and as the crew struggled to release the lifeboats; the bow disappeared beneath the surface, soon followed by the hull.*

Dialogue

Dialogue in fiction is not the speech of reality. Transcribed speech tends to be flat and boring. In a script, dialogue for actors has exposition, emotional states, differences in intensity, restricted points of view, and credibility issues. It sounds different and serves different purposes than in fictional stories. Dialogue in prose fiction must meet its responsibility to the storytelling, must be interesting, and may serve multiple purposes. These include exposition (description of basic facts), time orientation, scene placement, sensory perceptions, emotional states, conflict, characterization (how a character speaks, thinks, or feels), plot advancement, theme support, enlightenment (of character and reader), and others specific to the story that authors discover as they write.

Fiction dialogue must meet readers' expectations—expectations that become more exact as characterization and plot progress. Dialogue must also be appropriate for the story development and individual characters' personalities; the dialogue must seem real to the characters in their world.

> *"Is that a bear?" Joe asked.*
> *"Where?" Sam said.*
> *"Over there."*
> *"Damn. I think it is a bear."*
> *"What are we going to do?"*
> *"I don't know."*

In this example, there is no purpose to the multiple responses other than to call attention to the possibility of a bear being present. There is no plot advancement, no characterization, and imagery is not effective.

> *The bear reared back on its hind legs, roaring.*
> *"Don't move!" yelled Joe.*
> *"I'm going to throw up." Sam replied, sweat beading on his brow.*
> *"He's seen us."*
> *"I dropped my rifle."*
> *"Start making noise. Maybe we can scare him."*

This is better. It has elements of surprise, action, and characterization.

PRINCIPLES
-Dialogue should never be written to fill in or to replace essential facts or transitions. Each dialogue segment should serve multiple purposes. Dialogue should present only essential information for the story. For continuous story progression, dialogue should be spoken by the most effective character for the immediate story-related information and development.

-Modern dialogue in literary fiction is not effective as soliloquy, or sermon, or exposition of non-story-related facts. Dialogue must be in a consistent voice for the character and/or narrator.

Dialogue can be used to enhance oppressive narrative passages, but dialogue as boredom prevention is not effective.

-Dialogue must have a purpose related to the story and the character. Characters and narrators speaking in fiction must say only what they can reasonably be expected to think and formulate. A narrator's point of view may not be needed or useful in some stories, especially in the first person.

-The author's thoughts, feelings, opinions, or desires must not come through character dialogue. Authorial intrusions (in terms of voice, intellect, or personality) weaken effective character and narrator development, break the reader's involvement in the story, and rarely contribute to the story's development. This does not mean that a narrator's prevailing presence is not always in the story. Authors are of course always present in every story in a transparent, atmospheric way related to their individual style, storytelling capabilities, and writing skills and attitudes. Jane Austen's work will always be hers—she is there, transparent and as all-pervasive as the scent of dew-covered grass on a summer morn—but she is not in the drawing room with the characters or taking over the narrator's function.

-When creating dialogue in a fictional story, remember that the story world is created by the author with established parameters that the reader will agree with or stop reading. And dialogue, which will never be the way we talk in daily existence, must have certain rhythms, lengths, word choices, topics, and syntax that the reader will accept as part of the story world. Authors must keep within accepted parameters that multiply and solidify as the story progresses.

-Dialogue must not sound like actors in a stage play. Actors have different rules. Their speech has different rhythms and is more restricted.

-Dialogue must be constructed with attention to rhythmic effects that are consistent with the narrative and contribute to the reader's process. Excessively short bits of dialogue may create an unwanted "ping-pong" rhythm. In effective dialogue, a character's question or idea should rarely be answered directly. Modifiers used in attribution of dialogue should be tasteful. Avoid "'I love you,' he humorously chortled." Do not interject jolting, unrelated, or tangential ideas or speech inappropriate for the character .

GUIDELINES

-Test yourself: What is the purpose of your dialogue? Does it advance the story? Does it carry the action? Is it important in tone? Does it orient the reader? Does it contribute to characterization?

-Does the pace of your dialogue and the rhythm of the language provide a rich field for fictional voice development, show unique character thought patterns, and provide scene motion, often through attribution?

Voice

Voice is everything a character or narrator says and is affected by all thoughts and feelings in a story. Once voice is established for a character, the character's thoughts and words must respect that established voice. Each line spoken by a character must easily fit into all that has been thought and said by that character. Each character's voice, and the narrator's, must be consistent—or at least part of a predetermined progression of development—throughout the story.

Pay attention to the character or narrator's word choice, syntax, slang, ideation, opinion, and the length and complexity of sentences and phrases. Maintain story purpose (plot, characterization, significance) as a guide in developing distinctive voices. For instance, a character should not sound like a plantation slave of the nineteenth century just because the writer has the ear for that voice from a movie they recently saw.

Action

Stories must have action. The author uses dramatic structure to keep the story moving with conflict, action, and resolution, and keeps the reader in a defined story-present by minimizing recall and reflective discovery of past conflicts when they are not essential.

Stories in the main should be told in-scene and not predominantly via discursive narrative description. Readers are engaged by in-scene writing, but they are often denied the pleasure because narrative writing is easier for authors. Narrative writing lends itself to complicated, overextended, often irritating prose. "She crashed the party like a freight train without brakes," is less effective than "She entered the party uninvited, through the back door."

Consider these examples (with exaggerated prose to make a point) that illustrate differences between narrative description and in-scene writing:

> *Paul loved Helen but was jealous that she sang with so much passion that others couldn't take their eyes off her. She dreaded his obtuse sarcasm.*

Versus:

> *Helen held the floor-stand microphone with both hands. The piano player hunched over the keyboard and played the first notes. Helen took a deep breath and sang with a soft, breathy voice, her eyes closed until the refrain, when her gaze swept the audience of strangers, all riveted.*
>
> *She smiled, but refrained from taking a bow. The applause lasted more than a minute. Paul approached her as she left the stage.*
>
> *"I wish I could sing like that. All that emotion expressed so many times. We were almost in tears."*
>
> *"You obviously don't have my ear for perfection. Or my discrimination. It was an average performance."*
>
> *"It inflamed more than a few amorous thoughts."*
>
> *"I don't sing to evoke sexual advances."*
>
> *"You don't mean to."*
>
> *"Cut the bullshit, Paul. It's annoying."*

Language

Many authors have incomplete control of their language. Too often, the author of creative fiction assumes a level of competence in writing that is not sufficient to create a unique, lasting, worthwhile work of art.

Good writing requires:

- an exhaustive vocabulary
- egoless self-criticism

- storytelling excellence
- a rhythmic sense for creating effective prose
- logical punctuation
- perfect grammar

A writer must be caring and understanding of humanity and the special characteristics every human is given and develops to cope with our short existence in a complex and sometimes hostile, lonely world.

GUIDELINES

-Grammar is not just a set of rules intended to irritate creative types; it is the structure by which we write effective prose. It is a set of uniform, essential, language-specific guidelines that have been formed over centuries and are subject to continuous change. Correct spelling and grammar make reading easier and more fluid. Sloppy spelling and grammar are not stylistic; they are just amateurish. Rejecting grammar rules is only successful when the author possesses a total understanding of them. You must know the rules before you break them. You can't say you don't need grammar knowledge because you're great without it; readers will sense your shortcomings instinctively.

-Resist writing like others who are successful and admired. This is particularly true in revision. Write for clarity and effectiveness, and don't revise the text to sound more like the work of a famous author. Your writing must reflect you, and no one else.

Clichés are words and phrases that have been overused: "raining cats and dogs," "thunderous applause," "bottled-up emotions," and so on. An author must strive for fresh, vibrant language. Whether clichés are present is a judgment that depends on one's experience in reading and perception of the originality and vitality of any word or phrase. Experienced readers will notice and negatively judge clichés. Authors must remove deadening clichés from their writing.

Word choice must be accurate and deliberate. ("He held her in his arms," not "He crushed her in his arms.") Words must be appropriate to the context of the story and true to the narrative voice in action in the moment. Use a thesaurus; it's both necessary and fun. Finding the right word should give every author a touch of satisfaction.

disjunctive position of words and phrases will ever have more than a transient effect on the reader and will never create a lasting, memorable literary story. Great stories are about characters doing things that change their lives. The action is not just what happens from scene to scene; it's what emotions inside a character (inner story) drive him or her to the unique actions on the page (outer story) and the changes that result.

Value

A story must be worthy of the reader's involvement. The author must make the ideas, emotions, and action of the story force recognition or reversal in the character, and thus a significant stimulus to the reader's emotions so that the story will be remembered.

Suspense and mystery

All successful fiction is structured to make a reader curious about what happens next, what will be discovered. In literary fiction, suspense is also created when a reader worries about what will happen to a character they care about, what change will occur, how the character's life will be different.

Theme and Meaning

Theme: a distinct, recurring, unifying quality or idea

Meaning: a psychological or moral sense, purpose, or significance

Paradox: a statement that seems absurd or contradictory but may be true

Morality: standards of conduct that are accepted as right and proper

Hero: someone who acts with remarkable bravery, courage, or strength

Enlightenment: the state that results from having attained knowledge or insight

Epiphany: a moment of sudden revelation or insight

Stories create unique situations of unexpected, above-average happenings in believable and acceptable ways. We like heroes. And all fiction requires characters to have at least a touch of the heroic (showing courage or determination) to move the action of the story to its conclusion. Comatose people don't make good characters. But characters don't have to be hyperactive supermen, either; no need to recreate Ulysses, Gandhi, or Abraham Lincoln. But the best characters can, and usually do, have a part of the hero in them, and that heroic part engages the reader and drives the story forward.

PRINCIPLES

-In structuring a great story, theme and meaning need to be thoroughly explored in order to clarify the presentation and focus the enlightenment. Character recognition of something new and enlightening, and character reversal of thinking, intrigue the reader. Theme and meaning augment these effects.

-Heroism thrives when characters are put in difficult situations, and meaning is also enhanced in the heroic setting, because the actions of characters become more significant and often require strong morality. By thinking of heroic action, the author adds dimension to their writing.

-Morality dominates every fiction story, and the author's morality may be the same as, or different, from the narrator's. The differences can provide tension that results in stimulating prose. Character development is also related to the morality or the lack of morality in the characters' lives.

An author's thinking about morality and how it affects their writing will both consciously and unconsciously insert meaning into their stories. Such meaning, as it is defined and becomes easier for the reader to grasp, is always beneficial to the writing as a work of art. If the author thinks about the story extensively, themes and meanings may begin to develop early. A unifying theme does not have to be identifiable by the reader; even a subliminal theme may have a powerful effect.

But caution is needed: theme, morality, and meaning cannot be delivered with a heavy hand. Theme, morality, and meaning are like the taste of an elegantly prepared meal, which emerges from a blend of essential elements.

Good judgment must be pervasive. For example, moving characters through a story plot in order to express the author's opinion results in propaganda, and propaganda is not compatible with good fiction. Literary readers do not want to feel that the author's purpose is to persuade, even if they agree with the argument; readers want to be entertained and enjoy themselves.

GUIDELINES
-Think through characters' actions and conflicts in the story to see if there are sufficient recurrent ideas and motivations that logically contribute to the theme.

-Ask yourself whether the moral overlay of your writing is consistent for the story you are creating.

-Remember that paradoxes or contradictions can express both sides of an.issue and are useful in fiction but must be situated within a detailed and balanced presentation.

Distance

The narrator is telling the story. The story is not the world. Yet a story has a defined space, and the position of the reader in the story varies depending on the reader's relationship to the action. A reader can be given information close to the action, or far away from it.

Distance from the scene action can come into play when a narrator or character informs the reader of a distant or close perspective. The reader's distance from the action is created primarily through word choice (especially verbs and adverbs), type of images, character senses employed, and use of internal reflection. To diminish reader discomfort caused by shifts in the distance from the action requires attention to transitions and scene structures.

Through practice, writers will gain an instinctive sense of how to use distance of perspective in acceptable and pleasing ways. But not always. Consideration of distance in scenes is necessary when the scene is not working for best effect and the author is looking in revision to improve the reader's ease and sense of enjoyment.

Sentiment and sentimentality

Sentiment is a feeling or emotion; sentimentality is the tendency to indulge in emotion or nostalgia. For the author, sentimentality involves emotions not created through the interaction of believable characters in dramatic scenes. Sentimental writing uses stock images (so to speak) for emotion, and clichés for descriptions of character emotions, rather than the unique involvement of characters that makes the reader understand and share the characters' feelings.

Many readers seek sentimentality (some readers are perfectly happy with images of babies with wide eyes and dogs with wagging tails). Certain genres of fiction rely heavily on sentimentality: romance genre fiction, for instance, is built on sentimental clichés. But romance genre fiction is not a part of this discussion. In great art, the author must be able to create valid and credible emotional responses. The reader seeking higher levels of enjoyment will not accept the manipulation of feeling that sentimentality evokes.

Unfortunately for writers, perceiving sentimentality is subjective; there are no totally dependable rules. Understanding sentimentality in one's writing comes from experience in reading and writing, and from developing a better understanding of valid situations and characters that provoke emotions. Consider the following example of emotions demanded (via narrative) versus emotions implied (via in-scene drama):

> Narrative
> *The sight of the scruffy woman's sores as she held out her hand for money made Marcie want to cry.*

> In scene
> *The beggar sat cross-legged, reaching up with an open, shaking hand. The sores on her palm were wet and looked contagious. Marcie stepped back and took a dollar bill from her purse, dropping it toward the hand from a safe distance. The bill settled to the ground five feet from the beggar; a scruffy child lunged from the shadows of the highway overpass and disappeared with the gift. Marcie dug into her purse again and found a $20 bill, placed it in the beggar's hand, and walked away.*

CHAPTER 5

Revision

Revision should happen continuously while creating a story; it's not an end step in the writing process. Revision starts even before the writing begins, in a sense, since the essential thinking about the story cause and effect and credible characterization starts before a single word is committed to the page. Revision is important during the writing at all levels, from creating conflict and action to selecting the right word. Revision involves making changes in the story structure that will improve reader understanding and enjoyment, and it should be an essential part of an author's approach to storytelling.

PRINCIPLES

Entertain
Literary stories should be entertaining, and should enlighten or change existing thought.

Create
Writing *fiction* means creating a great story for the reader. Writing a *memoir* is telling with interest what has happened. To confuse your purpose decreases your effectiveness in each discipline. If memoir-related ideas are restricting your story, restructure.

Prose
Good storytelling depends on specific, not general, language; concrete, not abstract, ideas; fresh voice; character consistency; and avoidance of cuteness or self-importance.

Theme
Stories should have themes to create unity.

Freewill

Good modern stories avoid fatalism and predestination. Free will of the characters is what drives a literary story.

Backstory

Backstory (action or information that occurred before the story's beginning) is only effective as an integral part of a continuously progressing "front" story.

Time

Time and rhythm are embedded in characters' actions, the writing of the prose, and the act of reading. Time is linear, and a failure to orient the reader to time causes confusion.

Movement

Stories must have the potential for movement. Conflict is established, and then something happens.

Questions

Metaphysical questions may be posed by characters, the narrator, or the plot's dramatic structure. Resolutions to these question must answer everything the story poses, and nothing that occurs after the question is answered can change the story.

GUIDELINES. ASK:

Structure

When you read your work, are you engaged? Do you enjoy it? If you don't, even after hundreds of readings, your real-world reader has little chance of enjoying it the first time through. Look for ways to improve the structure of the story for tension and interest, more effective characterization, and increased drama. Simply generating multiple drafts doesn't necessarily result in good stories. Each successive draft must change and improve the story, not just meet a writing schedule. Make revisions effective by addressing structure and embedding what the reader needs to know and experience.

Elements

Are the fiction elements completely addressed for effect? Are priorities established and are they reasonable for story? Consider:

- prose
- characterization
- plot
- narration
- point of view
- setting
- imagery
- meaning/purpose
- drama

Character dimension
Have you fallen inadvertently into one-character and/or one dimensional storytelling, literal recall, too much internal reflection, unnecessary backstory, or excessive or awkward exposition?

Outline
Was your outline effective? If not, identify errors and look for ways to strengthen unity, coherence, theme, characterization, and time movement. When reviewing an outline, the drama should be inherently apparent and relate directly to story theme.

Scenes
Is the story told in dramatic scenes? Is drama ubiquitous, even in dialogue, in-scene action, and discursive narrative passages?

Themes
Are the themes clear? If not, restructure.

Drama
Is the essential conflict and resolution clear? Do all scenes have clear cause-and-effect?

Narrator
Have you considered your use of the narrator to create drama? Ineffective narrator conceptualization and use is a common error in literary storytelling as an art form. Is the story static because of your failure to involve a narrator?

Voice
Are characters' and narrator's voices vibrant and interesting?

Author
Are there spots in your writing where tone, voice, plot, or dialogue is dampened and ineffective because of a mental image or idea carried over from your own life experiences? If so, let your imagination revise.

Morality
Is there a consistent moral stance for the narrator and characters that is understandable to the reader? Are you able to create tension in the story and movement in the plot by using differences in moral attitudes?

Transitions
Are transitions elegant and dynamic? Are they relevant? Is the linking effective? Remember that line spaces, although useful, are not transitions.

Inner/outer story
If present, are your inner and outer stories balanced? A frequent error is too little outer story as compared to the inner story.

Perspective
Are there clear differences in perspective and diction (voice) between the narrator and the characters? Remember, a narrator usually tells a story that has already happened, and that is often different for the characters experiencing the story in story-time.

Freedom
Are there enough possibilities for the characters to act? This is essential to maintain the reader's belief in character and story.

Point of view
  Is the first-person point of view broad enough? Don't be afraid to expand the first-person character's view of the story—but keep the character credible. Although it can be difficult to make seamless for the reader so that no rupture in smooth telling occurs, a richer worldview in first-person POV often provides maximum story impact.

  Have you stayed in a close point of view for so long that the story collapses? For example, "Tony saw the envelope on the desk, the crooked stamp, the scruffy corners. Pale blue, too, the color

Maggie always loved. And her handwriting! The cramped tails on the y's, the o's like pinholes, the r's flattened to almost straight lines. In a thousand years he could never mistake this writer." Revise by cutting.

Characters
Have you lost characters? Keep track of all characters—where they are, what they are thinking, what they're doing—even though most of that information will never be in the story.

Reader
Have you provided too much the reader didn't want to know (setting detail, recall, reflection)? Have you provided too little of what readers want to know (characterization)?

Length
Are your scenes longer in the middle than at the beginning or end? Keep a good balance and meet reader expectations with pleasure and surprise.

Narrator
Have you created the best voice for the narrator? Avoid sloppy or cute diction. And don't limit the narrator's intelligence.

Have you avoided too much narrator commentary on the characters? For example, "Jamie did not like ice cream. He didn't like Brussels sprouts, either. In truth, he was relatively intolerant of all foods."

Does the narration smother the characters? Excessive telling may swamp required character action.

Does the narrator come too close to the characters? The reader should never have a sense that a character has taken over the storytelling. Characters are too busy being themselves and carrying the story action to provide narrator-type ideas and details.

Withheld information
Have you withheld crucial story information from the reader to create tension? You should give the reader everything he or she needs to know about story progression. Withholding information is a technique to

create mystery and suspense in fiction, but in literary fiction, the most useful suspense is when the reader wonders what will happen to a character they care about.

Psychology

Have you indulged in psychoanalysis? Stories are not essays on psychology. Dramatize psychological ideas.

APPENDIX

Excellence in Literary Storytelling:
Discover Your Reasons for Writing

Successful authors of literary fiction must have clarity of mind regarding who they are and why they write. The telling of fictional stories is a performance that can be damaged or destroyed by ill-conceived attitudes about writing. When writing stories in literary fiction, authors may reveal traits of self that are unacknowledged or unrecognized—egotism, conceit, arrogance, narcissism—that prohibit character development. Ask yourself:

Do I write to continue to master the skills of writing as an art form—truly a lifelong process? Or do I write stories to explain my own experienced emotions and thereby feel better about myself (and try to prove I am an author)?

Great stories are dramatically constructed art forms—sculptures in words—that produce enlightened change in characters and readers. Stories are not just flamboyant descriptions of lived abstractions such as love, hate, revenge, or jealousy. Authors create stories that engage and change readers. And authors must not use descriptive narrative in attempts to purge themselves of emotional or intellectual crises. The object of great writing is not therapeutic self-discovery.

Am I striving to tell a creative fictional story based on my own imagination, or am I writing a memoir or biography as fiction in which I describe characters and past events?

Memoir is a popular and legitimate form of writing, but writing a memoir requires skills that often conflict with imaginative fiction. Adherence to the truth of what happened, and/or the belief that a story based on true events or real people is equal or superior to the created fictional story, are destructive convictions for a writer intent on writing effective fictional stories. Most great stories are not simply told from life; great stories are ideas (that may be stimulated by life) successfully expressed through a dramatic, significant series of fictional events.

Do I write for creative excellence, or to replicate the fame and fortune of celebrated writers?

All authors want recognition for their work, but that recognition should be for writing lasting, memorable stories that entertain and enlighten. A desire for fame imposes restrictions on the creation of a great story and will never satisfy a fiction writer's dreams of success in creating high-caliber, widely admired fiction. Writing a fictional story is a selfless process. Egoistic writing and storytelling of poor quality masquerading as literary fiction cannot be promoted to the uninformed as worthy just to satisfy a writer's quest for fame (and a publisher's for profit). If a writer's literary fiction is of quality and will survive in future generations, it must be written with altruistic intentions.

Do I write to provide significant theme and meaning through entertainment and enlightenment, or to persuade readers to agree with some presumption or opinion?

To persuade a reader to a particular authorial opinion often does not support the creation of a great story, and rarely lasts in the minds of literary readers. Literary fiction is about people as characters—characters who may ponder metaphysical questions, experience passionate emotions, and participate in politics or the search for scientific truth, for example—but who, through their emotional and intellectual complexity and acting with a constant moral compass and durable intellect, create interest and momentum through objective narration of a significant story written by a skillful, imaginative author. Fiction authors enlighten about human nature; essayists, editorialists, and columnists persuade readers to form opinions. Fiction authors who insert unrelated opinions in their stories are actually creating propaganda—deceptive or distorted information about policy, ideas, doctrines, or causes—that deviates from the truth required for significant fiction.

Do I revise to improve story quality, readability, and characterization, or do I revise to impress a reader with my authorial intellect and cleverness?

Literary stories fail because of ineffective characterization; incredible, incomprehensible conflicts and actions; or lack of readability. Stories rarely fail because the prose is insufficiently erudite or overwrought. Authors must write to be easily understood, and make their prose logical, credible, and significant in enlightening understanding of the human soul. There must be a purpose in the story and a unified structure. Too many authors revise through exhaustive prose adjustment in style and craft, when, for success in writing literary fiction, valuable revision emerges from: 1) structural adjustment, 2) clarity of purpose in the writing throughout, 3), mastery of craft, manifest in the provision of emotional and intellectual change in characters and the reader, and 4) devotion to clear ideas that are compatible and lead to coherent story plot and characterization.

Do I believe stories are dramatic events rich with ideas for a reader to experience, or just written words for the reader to interpret?

Fictional stories entertain and enlighten through drama: conflict, action, and resolution. Readers do not simply observe a great fictional story; they become involved in it. The writer's challenge is to engage the reader from the story's beginning to its end, not just to describe loosely connected or unrelated events. Successful writers provide only enough information to stimulate the story's meaning and momentum in the reader's mind. An engaged reader's story interpretation is unique to each reader and determined by that reader's intelligence, experience, empathy, and creativity.

Do I believe that stories are structures whose unity is discovered as the reader progresses, or that they are meandering observations described haphazardly, avoiding unity, continuity, or cause and effect?

Authors who start a character on a plotline, wondering what he or she might turn out to do, limit themselves. Stories are carefully constructed as the writing progresses and offer up carefully chosen details that create images and ideas in the mind of the reader. Authors who insist on an unstructured approach and write scenes without intentionality will fail to deliver true reader enjoyment.

Other Books by William H. Coles
McDowell
Guardian of Deceit
The Surgeon's Wife
The Spirit of Want
Sister Carrie
Facing Grace with Gloria and Other Stories
The Necklace and Other Stories
Story in Literary Fiction: A Manual for Writers
Literary Fiction as an Art Form: A Text for Writers
The Short Fiction of William H. Coles 2001-2011
The Illustrated Fiction of William H. Coles 2000-2012